First published in 2020

ISBN: 978-1-951171-07-0

Published by:
Tank Archives Press

PO Box 181802
Coronada, CA 92178, USA

Editor: Bruce Oliver Newsome, PhD.

THEY SOUGHT OUT ROMMEL

A diary of the Libyan Campaign, from November 16th to December 31st, 1941

THE ARMY AT WAR

LONDON
HIS MAJESTY'S STATIONERY OFFICE
1942

LIBYA is full of our troops. It is grand. Everywhere there are eager faces ; convoy commanders sitting up aloft their trucks like sunburned gods—their sun compasses pointing a black sliver of shadow towards the Boche ; despatch riders bumping incredibly through the sandy, rutted tracks ; officers in groups, their maps on knees, listening to their orders ; lorried infantry waiting, waiting, waiting ; guns, their dust covers off, marching through the infantry and off to a flank in majestic indifference.

List of Abbreviations

A.B.	Armoured Brigade
A.D. Armd. Div. }	Armoured Division
Adv. H.Q.	Advanced Headquarters
Army Ops.	Army Operations
A.T.B.	Army Tank Brigade
Bde.	Brigade
B.G.S.	Brigadier, General Staff
B.M.	Brigade Major
C.I.H.	Central Indian Horse
C.O.	Commanding Officer
Coy.	Company
Don R.	Despatch Rider
Fd.	Field
Gds.	Guards
G.1	General Staff Officer, Grade 1
G.S.I.	General Staff Intelligence
h.e.	high explosive
I.C.E.	Individual Compass Error
Ind. Div.	Indian Division
Infy. Infty. }	Infantry
I.O.	Intelligence Officer
I-tank	Infantry Tank
K.D.G.'s	King's Dragoon Guards
km.	kilometres
L.A.D.	Light Aid Detachment
L. of C.	Line of Communication
m.	miles
M. & V.	Meat and Vegetables
m.g.	machine-gun
M.T.	Motor Transport
N.Z.	New Zealand
25-pdrs.	25-pounders
P.O.W.	Prisoner of War
P.R.	Public Relations
recce.	reconnaissance
recced.	reconnoitred
Regt.	Regiment
S.A.	South African
Tks.	Tanks
U.P.	United Press

Sketch maps of the campaign on pp. 8 and 12.

THEY SOUGHT OUT ROMMEL

Sunday, Nov. 16that P.R. Camp, Bagush

There is battle in the air; I swear there is. It lies thick on the palate. From strictly official quarters there is no word yet, though pretty well all the newspaper men have arrived in camp here and are—more or less—straining at the leash.

For days now the traffic along the road a mile away had been enormously increased. Everything moving up. The New Zealand people, almost next door to the camp, moved out two days ago without any fuss or bother. I saw them go; a good lot—virile, strong, a bit bigger all round than our Tommies and without their pertness and everlasting grin.

Great sweeps of fighters wheeling overhead and lots of bombers; also, some Bombays—old bombers now used for other purposes.

Sam Brewer, *Chicago Tribune*, Matt Halton, *Toronto Star*, and Alaric Jacob, *Reuters*, form my team of reporters for battle.

Hours of checking and re-checking stores and kit and going over the M.T. against a sudden order to move. Maps, talcs, compass, glasses, arms and ammunition, food (we have an almighty store and some very special specialities in tins), and, most important, water.

Left Bagush in good time having seen all other parties except two off and properly equipped. Made Adv. Army H.Q. at Piccadilly, where we also have an Adv. H.Q., and swopped over one of my trucks, the 15-cwt. Bedford which sprang a leak in the radiator and nearly reduced me to tears by using precious water as if it were a hungry Russian eating caviar at a wedding feast.

Not much news of what is happening ahead, except that 30th Corps is due inside Libya early to-morrow. This is a grand thought. We must be with them.

Sam cooks the stew gallantly in great difficulties, meanwhile everyone is soaked.

TUESDAY, 18 NOV. 41 *On Frontier Wire*
N. of Maddalena

All day we chased 30th Corps across the desert and finally had to give it up and camp here with 13th Corps. A devilish day. We set off early and then spent hours nosing around through the worst sand-storm I have ever been in; a real brute. Met up with a mass of other parties, all of whom were in the same boat—mostly photographers. They attached themselves to me—a gesture of confidence which was flattering but distinctly nerve-racking—and finally around midday I landed in an advanced R.A.A.F. fighter H.Q. and met up with a padre. He told me where 30th Corps was headed (though God alone knows how he knew). They are 30 miles on into Libya. Great stuff, though infuriating, since there was not a hope of catching them—for the moment, anyhow.

At 14.00 hrs. made 13th Corps who were just about to shuffle off West. B.G.S. gave me an idea of the general situation; our tanks are through the wire and gunning for the Boche, setting, it seems, a course pretty well due West along the line of the Trigh el Abd, an old caravan

route which joins a number of others at El Gubbi, 60 km.
due South of Tobruk.

Part of the 4th Ind. Div. and an Infy. Bde.—with
some I-tanks moving North up the wire with their eyes
on Sidi Omar, where, I remember, we did some hearty
work last June.

Thank heavens we are leaving Hellfire Pass and Sollum
alone for the time being. There are more mines to the
square yard up there than I like to think about. It is
logical to suppose that our mobile forces will get in and
behind the frontier posts, and fight across the Boche L. of
C., and then deal with these birds at Hellfire and Sollum
later.

Passed through the New Zealand Div. on our way
here. Their transport stretches right across the desert
to the South; extraordinarily impressive. Bren carrier
crews snatching sleep rolled up in their blankets against
the tractors. Imagine they will do a night march to be
resting so early.

It is exhilarating to be as near enemy territory as this;
and, bless them, the R.A.F. are already most calmly
installed alongside with fighters taking off every five
minutes and ripping through the deepening haze to
Libya. Nothing seen of enemy at all, air force or otherwise, though there is some banging about up North—
gunfire and a little m.g. fire.

What grips one here is the calmness and confidence of
everyone.

My chickens wrote their stories and I checked over the
trucks and equipment and then made stew. Announced
that water ration would be two pints per man per day for
all purposes; we have to be completely self-contained
for 14 days minimum. All personnel to shave daily;
correct desert travel formation to be maintained at all
times; tyres to be checked at every halt; petrol, oil and
mileage to be logged by drivers each night irrespective

of my log ; talc maps to be kept in my car where I have a small tin of petrol for their destruction should this be necessary ; no diaries except this (easily burnable) to be kept.

Have twice re-checked I.C.E. of my compass and now we are all set to go into Libya to-morrow at first light.

19 Nov. 41   *50 m. Inside Libya*

At 14.35 hrs., after a long and weary chase, finally caught up with 30th Corps. The first 20 miles across Libya were tricky ; no tracks, of course, and one did not quite know where the Boche was. It was hot and there were mirages of the most disturbing sort !—though most of them, I fancy, were of the mind.

Saw a great, unending line of transports moving slowly across our front roughly four miles distant and recced. it with the utmost care through the glasses before finding it to be our own and feeling a trifle self-conscious and over-careful.

A grounded Tomahawk had a cheery South African pilot sitting in the shade of the wing contentedly munching bully. We said, Did he need any help, and he said, No, he was all right and that the motor of his machine had got all temperamental.

Libya—this part of it, anyhow—is full of our troops. It is grand. Everywhere there are eager faces ; convoy commanders sitting up aloft their trucks like sunburned gods—their sun compasses pointing a black sliver of shadow towards the Boche ; despatch riders bumping incredibly through the sandy, rutted tracks ; officers in groups, their maps on knees, squatting on their hunkers listening to their orders ; lorried infantry waiting, waiting, waiting ; guns, their dust covers off, marching through the infantry and off to a flank in majestic indifference, one somehow thinks, to all ordered plans.

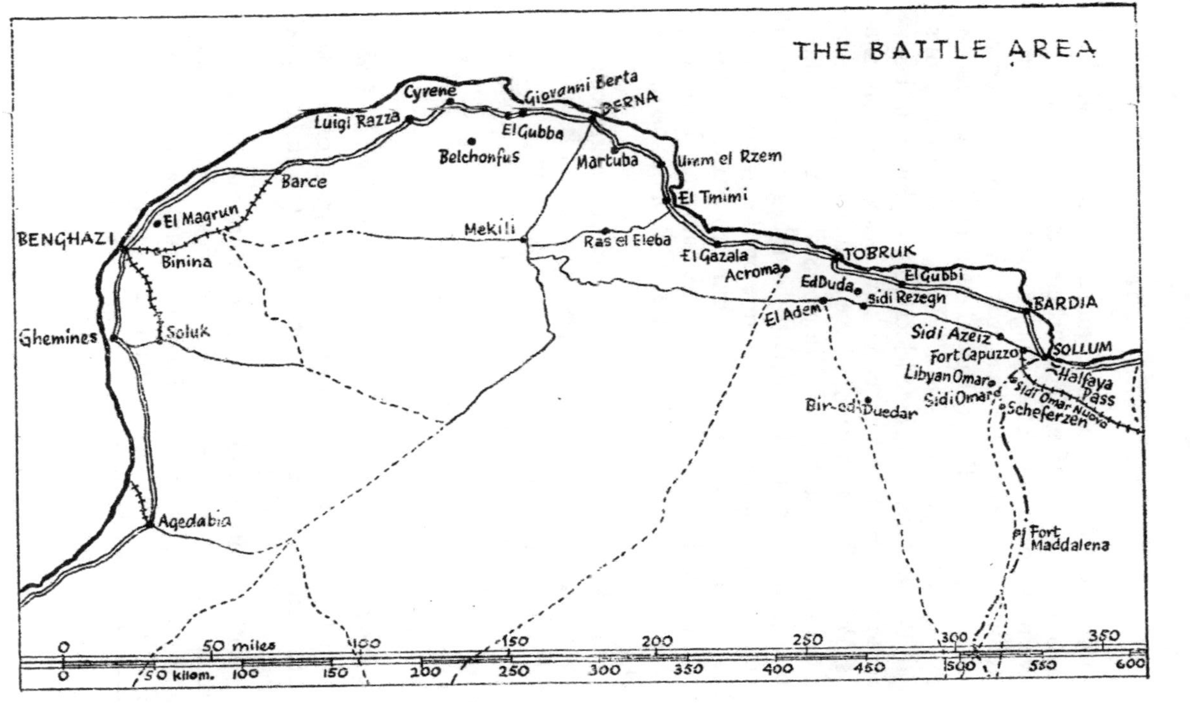

THE BATTLE AREA
Cyrene
Giovanni Berta
DERNA
Luigi Razza
El Gubba
Belchonfus
Martuba
Umm el Rzem
Barce
El Tmimi
BENGHAZI
El Magrun
Mekili
Ras el Eleba
El Gazala
TOBRUK
Binina
Acroma
El Gubbi
Ed Duda
sidi Rezegh
BARDIA
El Adem
Ghemines
Soluk
Sidi Azeiz
Fort Capuzzo
SOLLUM
Libyan Omar
Halfaya Pass
Sidi Omar Nuovo
Bir ed Duedar
Sidi Omar
Scheferzen
Agedabia
Fort Maddalena
50 miles
100
150
200
250
300
350
50 kilom.
100
150
200
250
300
350
400
450
500
550
600

30th Corps' Armoured Command vehicles, wireless masts waving like fronds on their flexible mountings, have now come into close laager for the night and the Intelligence people state that Adv. Army has moved to Maddalena. The Boche has fallen back in the general direction of Tobruk—North-West, that is—and his 15th Panzer Div. is believed located with his main body there; no news of his second armoured division, the 21st Panzer Div. Our tanks have contacted some at least of the Italian Ariete South-West of Sollum and knocked out 12 M.13 tanks. The R.A.F. have bagged 36 planes one way and another—quite a few on the ground; and Beaufighters, of which we had hitherto heard nothing, appeared to have done most of the damage. Later on, there is news of a tank battle at El Gubbi but no details yet.

For many reasons, chiefly those of wireless silence and the extreme mobility of the opposing forces, it is difficult to get a complete picture of what is happening.

El Gubbi looks a good bet for to-morrow, I should say.

20 Nov. 41 *In front of El Gubbi*

First taste of real war to-day. Spent most of the day with 30th Corps and then set course (23 m. on 344 degrees) for El Gubbi.

With about 10 miles to go, came up with 1st South African Div., who had run into a sticky time, one way and another, with Stukas and other pests of a like nature. Pushed on. I was so intent on keeping a correct course that I failed to appreciate that, very soon, the numbers of trucks and men and so forth were getting fewer. The desert was good and we were speeding in grand style. Then, out of the corner of my eye, I saw an officer waving frantically. Stopped, thinking he wanted a lift. He said, " Do you propose to take El Gubbi with those three vehicles ? " and I said No, we didn't care about taking it if someone else wanted the honour. " Well," he said, " in that case you had better not go any further ; this is the front line."

There was no doubt about it two minutes later. A flock of Stukas came over and smartened things up a bit. They were followed by some G.50's machine-gunning, and then the artillery took a hand just to show there was no ill-feeling.

Not much damage was done and it was agreed, any-how, that it was a good thing to have a sample of each of these delights in quick time so that they should be known for what they were.

Round and about are many Italian tanks and some of ours. All very badly shot up and some with their dead still in them. The oddest details remain in one's mind. The commander of one Wop tank, lying dead beside his machine, had his fingers crossed ; and he had absurdly small feet cased in new boots.

Gather that we got 36 of their tanks here. El Gubbi is defended in force by, we believe, the Wops and there are a good many tanks floating around ; one can see them occasionally through the glasses.

This bit of country is held by one S.A. Bde.

It seems that the 22nd Armoured Bde. (caught sight of their Bde. H.Q. as we were coming through) were in the hooley here yesterday and that now they are shifting round to our right flank and going on due North towards Tobruk.

Dusk is falling now and these tatty G.50's are back again machine-gunning. Matt Halton is in the un-enviable position of sharing a slit-trench with an officer who is using his (Matt's) shoulder as a rest for his rifle while he has a poop at the Wops. I can see him wince every time the thing goes off; it must nearly shatter his ear-drums.

Cold and rather damp.

NIGHT 20/21

There is a terrific battle on somewhere. Hour after hour of gunfire.

It is very cold. Some movement of transport, and well before first light a machine-gun Coy. came lurching through us feeling its way like a clumsy elephant through the slit-trenches and bad ground. The men are dark splotches; occasionally a far-off flare throws off a thin gleam from a rifle barrel; there are soft orders in Afrikaans, sometimes repeated in harsher, grimmer tones; the gear-boxes of the lorries groan and whine, hesitate and go on; and in our beds we turn and shiver. With cold. The guns over to the North-East still bang away. Fairly light stuff; anti-tank maybe.

21 NOV. 41 *Back at 30th Corps*

Shellfire, machine-gunning and dive-bombing pinned us to the ground for a long time. Not very big shells, not very determined machine-gunning (Wop planes) and not very accurate dive-bombing. Uncomfortable, of course, and irritating because we wanted to get away and see what was happening to the rest of the battle.

Once a great crowd of our fighters came over escorting a tight, prim herd of Marylands and soon, far off, came great gouts of dust and spume from the Marylands' bombs, most of them with angry black centres, telling of hits on vehicles. They look damned businesslike. While this was going on, some Boche 109's came over on a parallel course (opposite direction, of course) escorting Stukas—first time I'd seen such a thing.

So there was the spectacle of either side doing much

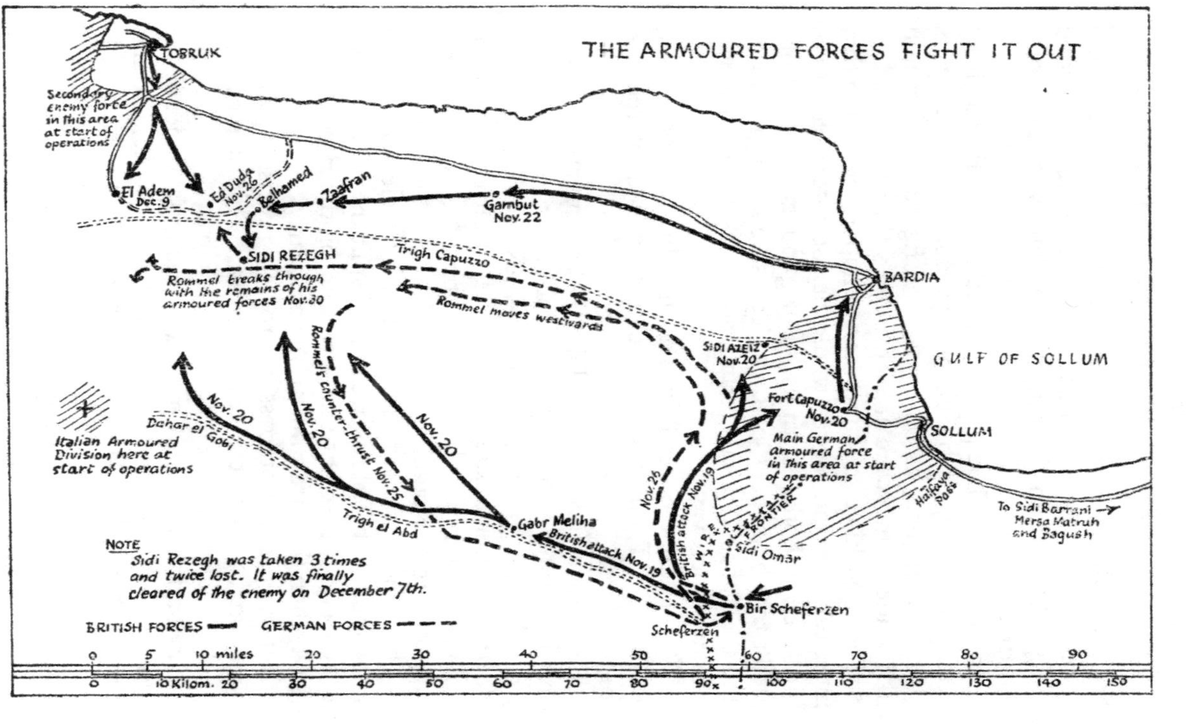

THE ARMOURED FORCES FIGHT IT OUT
TOBRUK
Secondary enemy force in this area at start of operations
El Adem Dec. 9
Ed Duda Nov. 26
Belhamed
Zaafran
Gambut Nov. 22
SIDI REZEGH
Trigh Capuzzo
Rommel breaks through with the remains of his armoured forces Nov. 30
Rommel moves westwards
BARDIA
SIDI AZEIZ Nov. 20
GULF OF SOLLUM
Nov. 20
Dahar el Gobi
Nov. 20
Rommel's counter-thrust Nov. 25
Nov. 20
Fort Capuzzo Nov. 20
Main German armoured force in this area at start of operations
SOLLUM
Italian Armoured Division here at start of operations
Trigh el Abd
Gabr Meliha
British attack Nov. 19
Nov. 26
British attack Nov. 19
W. I. R. E.
FRONTIER
Sidi Omar
Halfaya Pass
To Sidi Barrani Mersa Matruh and Bagush
NOTE
Sidi Rezegh was taken 3 times and twice lost. It was finally cleared of the enemy on December 7th.
Bir Scheferzen
Scheferzen
BRITISH FORCES
GERMAN FORCES
0 5 10 miles 20 30 40 50 60 70 80 90
0 10 Kilom. 20 30 40 50 60 70 80 90 100 110 120 130 140 150

the same thing. I thought, when they've finished and start back, then they'll meet and that should be a good party. This from the far, far too shallow bottom of a slit-trench.

It happened. The parties slid past each other as if by arrangement; each bunch of fighters saw off safely its charges and then, as on signal, the fighters tore round like wildcats and were at each other's throats.

Thought this a good moment to hop it, reckoning that most earth-bound blokes would be too interested in the bird-men to bother with us. But gunners of all nations aren't that human. Our Long Toms kept banging away and the Wops kept answering, so it was between salvos that we got away.

We passed the dead Italian with his fingers crossed again. So I uncrossed mine and cursed myself for forgetfulness.

Set course for 1st S.A. Div. H.Q., missing another dive-bombing attack by about a mile; learned that 5th S.A. Bde. are driving up towards Sidi Rezegh, due North and immediately below the eastern perimeter of Tobruk. Our people there are breaking out, as one supposed they would.

The general strategy becomes a little clearer. If we link hands with Tobruk we should split the enemy forces in two, and if they have their armour on the East of such a link, then they are sunk good and hearty.

But it just is not possible to tell precisely what is happening. Distances are so great. Things move so quickly. Information is hard to come by.

Navigation to 30th Corps was tricky (a puncture *en route* and constant boiling of one truck engine) and the country bad. But landed plumb on the target, which earned some praise—small beer beside my own relief.

Anyone who says navigation in the desert is easy is talking through his tin hat.

Met Churchill at Corps and he told of an old friend, Bob Crisp, the S.A. Test cricketer, knocking out a couple of tanks with two shots. Pretty good bowling ; but then the boy always was a bit quick off the pitch.

Made a terrific stew and now have a distended stomach and a cold in the head.

22 Nov. 41   *With 30th Corps*

Desperately anxious for news of the Tobruk sortie, hung around Corps most of the day and then moved with them to astride the Trigh el Abd, by which time it was too late for us to push on, as I had intended to contact either 5th S.A. Bde. or 7th Armoured Div., both of whom must be having quite a party, I should think.

But news, news, news, real news of what is happening is short to-day, though I feel in my bones that big things are happening up North there.

Had a prolonged food, water and M.T. check-up. Tested compass, checked maps and bits and pieces. Also had a crack at a couple of bounding gazelle in the hope of snaffling a little fresh meat. Hostilities ceased in favour of the gazelle, which, Sam said, ran faster than the Wops.

23 Nov. 41   *With 7th Armd. Div. Adv. H.Q.*

With not too clear an idea where they were, we set out for 7th A.D. Got 12 miles on the way and ran into the rather battered remnants of a Bn. of an Armoured Bde. carting along 300 Boche and 300 Wop prisoners and towing some tanks.

They did not reckon on having many runners left (tank people always refer to machines still in good order as " runners ") but were full of teeth and hair.

God made these people and they are British. I suppose

He made the Boche also, but it seems a grievous sort of error : a mistake of some kind.

For an hour we stopped and talked to them and heard of great deeds. The position forward is still confused and they could not, in the general sense, help us much about it. But oh, my heart !—they told of such doings, so simply, so much without affectation, so much as good people tell their tales.

A shy one-pipper was jollied by his pals into telling how he had gone into battle with the cruiser tanks in a dingo (a tiny, part-armoured runabout that would not stop a rabbit's charge) loosing off his Bren gun like old boots and having the whale of a time. Finally some earnest Boche took a moment off to fire something at him and knocked out the dingo. Great tanks were furiously grinding about him and every gun in the world was going bang, so he sat on a tufty sand-bush and loosed off his pistol at any old hole in a Boche tank that appeared to have anything inside it. Night came and he was alone among a lot of dead and a general shambles. So he lay in a shallow slit-trench which the Wops had used as a lats. And in the night got away, walked 11 miles, found his own people and was there, dodging the C.O. who was likely to ask awkward questions about the loss of his runabout !

On general form, gathered that our link with the Tobruk people had been broken and that terrific scrapping was going on forward. Also, an unpleasantly large amount of Boche armour reported ahead, slap on our course. Well, this was tricky. Our people said they were withdrawing for a spell, so it did not seem the best idea in the world to barge ahead.

Anyhow, I spotted a staff car with armoured car escort bounding in our direction and hurled my three vehicles in its wake, hoping to get some idea of what was happening from the staff car occupants, whoever they might be. Finally pulled up among the rear bits of the S.A. Bde. (our old pals from El Gubbi who had been replaced there by a Support Group, I believe) and found the occupant of the staff car to be the Commander of a S.A. Div. He did not stay there long, and said he was shoving off to A.D.—our destination—so we followed him and met there old friends.

Cannot say that the S.A. Bde. seemed too happy about things, for there seemed a lot of armour in front of them, which meant that they could not push on *immediately*— the one thing that they simply revel in doing. They hate sitting on their bottoms. They want to be up and at the enemy and deep into his vitals, striking with their strong right arms. But you cannot fight armour with infantry.

As soon as we arrived at 7th A.D., two dog-fights claimed the sky above. The machines were very high and I am blessed if I could tell who was who; two machines came down—the pilot of one baling out and landing some miles away.

A crashing machine always gives me an odd sensation; for some stupid reason I expect it to bounce when it hits the ground. It never does. There is just an almighty cloud of smoke and flame, and one man who can always see better than anyone else saying, " That was one of theirs—saw the marking."

It is getting dark now. A frantic battle is going on in the direction of the S.A. Bde.—lots of 25-pdrs. fire, lots of tank and anti-tank fire also. There is a good deal of firing up towards Sidi Rezegh area.

Constantly it is this way. I suppose we are in as good a position as anyone—better than most—to know what is going on ; yet here are these battles in progress and for all we know it might be the Chinese fighting the Japs ; except that it isn't. It is the British fighting the Germans, at last on something like equal terms, and we are hammering the living hell out of them. I dare say they are fighting well. It is silly and inaccurate to suppose that they are not good soldiers; they are; but we are better.

24 Nov. 41   *A.D. Adv. H.Q.*

For the first time in six days we have an opportunity to sit back and consider things at leisure, while waiting for the Commander of 30th Corps to see us. It is a little after 10.00 hrs. The day is brilliantly fine and warm and I have discarded the balaclava helmet that has given me such comfort—especially when sleeping.

There is some desultory banging about. Information is that yesterday's late afternoon battle went fairly well, though all reports are not yet in. 100 Boche tanks took a crack at the S.A. Bde. and ran on to Support Group while the Armd. Bde. took them in the flank. They were strong enough to go on into and through the S.A. Bde. position and among their B Echelon, where the most unpleasant shindy went on.

It occurs to me that our left flank must now be somewhat precarious. But one does not have the full picture yet.

From what I can gather, the Boche, seeing our grand move early on, cracked the corridor between our Southern forces and the Tobruk sortie, and so far we have not been able to re-establish the corridor. The New Zealanders and some support from the Tank Bde. with I-tanks came whizzing along the line of the Trigh Capuzzo from East to West in an attempt to join up again, but they do not seem to have been able to make it.

So, I would say, things do look a trifle sticky, unless we have so battered his armour in this last free-for-all that he cannot now go on; depends on how many tanks the rats have and how good their recovery has been.

Recovery is the real strength of an armoured division. No tank is finished until it is burnt out ; just to *knock* them out is not sufficient, because highly efficient recovery-sections are on the job in a flash and doing their refurbishing in no time. The Boche even have their recovery-sections in battle, lugging the knocked-out machines away while the fun and games is still in progress.

As I write this rather ponderous, Johnny-Know-All stuff, the battle still rages all round us.

I think a nice cup of tea would go down well ; also, a check up all round once more. The drivers get rather browned-off at my constant check-ups, I know, but I am an uneasy soul in these matters.

MIDDAY

Some Crusaders (cruiser tanks) are haring in this direction looking a bit the worse for wear. Gunfire on the left flank has been increasing and getting steadily nearer. Some M.T. movement visible in that direction through the glasses.

FROM THE LOG

Time	Remarks	Mileage
12.10	Heavy and sustained shellbursts on bearing 235 degrees.	
12.13	Heavier shellbursts 235 degrees, less than 1 m. distant.	
12.14	Under way. Course 118 degrees.	4494.2
12.18	Change course to 145 degrees.	4494.9
12.56	Rear truck bursts tyre.	4500.1
13.16	Under way. Course 140 degrees.	

From the Log—*continued.*

Time	Remarks	Mileage
14.24	Change course to 160 degrees.	4511.0
15.03	Halt for pin-pointing. Map ref. 475 347.	4521.9
17.05	Crossed wire Scheferzen into Egypt. Course 30 degrees.	4537.9
17.45	Halt.	4541.2
18.30	Under way. Course due North.	
21.10	Halt. Planes dropping flares.	4543.7
22.43	Under way.	
01.45	Halted. Head of convoy in minefield.	
02.10 to 03.45	Under way. Constant stops. Many flares and enemy Very lights. Three crashes ; all vehicles damaged ; one leaking badly in radiator. Main body convoy lost. Refound.	
04.25	Proceeded through minefield after halt. Rear truck bursts tyre ; abandoned.	
05.00	Attempted rejoin convoy.	
06.15	Halted ; waited for dawn ; turned back and found abandoned truck ; repaired puncture.	
07.00 to 07.35	Shelled.	4556.0

25 Nov. 41   *Sidi Omar Nuovo*

It is now almost midnight. Writing by tiny torch glimmer in the blackout truck. This has been a horrible 36 hrs. I feel a little sick with fatigue, dust and sand and cordite fumes, as, I am certain, the rest of the party (now bedded down) do.

Not easy to get things in their proper sequence but the log helps.

Clearly the old Boche has counter-attacked in no mean style, and in this sector, anyhow, we are back on our heels and there must be the hell of a lot of confusion about.

A few minutes after the Crusaders came into 7th A.D. Adv. H.Q., we moved off bag and baggage while gunfire on the left flank grew steadily nearer. Everything very orderly, but, hang it, the gunfire to the flank *followed us*. It could only have been tanks or highly mobile guns. Very soon it was clear that he must have broken through at the El Gubbi position and launched a frontal attack from Sidi Rezegh at the same time. The desert was one seething mass of our transport. All soft stuff, of course, which is money for jam to tanks and can do nothing but beat it when unsupported. Mostly B Echelon.

Kept on the tail of our main column and then, goddam it, the rear of my three trucks punctured. Got to work on it and meanwhile moved most valuable kit to other trucks—just in case. Soon we were alone except for one lonely wireless truck half a mile to our right, which was observing and reporting on the attacking column. He was on a slight rise and I gave orders to clear out when he did, even if the wheel had not been changed.

We were just finishing when the wireless truck buzzed off in a swelter of dust and sand, being smartened up by some h.e. and (probably, unless they were duds) some solid shot as well.

Simply could not bring myself to leave the truck, so cursed everyone to greater activity. We made it. I thought most people looked a bit relieved and hate to think how I looked.

Had no clear idea, of course, where 7th A.D. had gone, so decided the best thing to do was to set a course for the frontier wire at roughly Scheferzen and then see what the form was. After a time, the guns still banging away monotonously on the flank but never getting close in, thank heavens, ran into a large New Zealand convoy with 300 drab, weary-looking Boche prisoners in the trucks.

And then, across the desert, came racing a black truck with at least nine people aboard, three of them clinging to the running-board and mudguards. They were War Photographers; two of them, Bayliss of *Paramount* and Noble of *Universal*, had lost their car. The wretched thing punctured when they were being chased by enemy tanks and they had to run for it. The people with them had turned back, piled them on somehow and brought them to safety—well, out of immediate range, anyhow.

On again with them following me, and once more caught up with a desert full of our transport. I could have choked with rage that so soon we should have to back-pedal, but consoled myself with the knowledge that we simply had to do this in order to re-form and get the Boche by the short hairs again. Nevertheless, it was saddening.

At dusk we hit the frontier wire while our fighters screamed overhead in protection at the bottle-neck through the wire.

Halted; went on at snail's pace; halted; Boche Very lights soaring up through the night's darkness on three sides; knew we *must* be headed for the minefields surrounding Sidi Omar; planes droning overhead and dropping whacking great flares, lighting everything up in clearest detail; might have been ours—they did not bomb us, anyhow. On again after a conference. Then the head of the convoy charged slap into a minefield and by the grace of the Almighty failed to blow itself up.

Tricky business getting out.

The moon was up. The convoy moved in jerks. Three times we crashed into cars ahead or were crashed into by those behind. Almost impossible to see in the whirling, choking clouds of sand and dust.

At a junction the convoy got split ; driver of the truck twelve ahead of mine went to sleep at the wheel, woke and drove on like fury straight ahead, whereas, in fact, he should have turned left (as I afterwards discovered) through the gap in the minefield.

We were lost for a time. Bayliss and I re-formed convoy, led it back on foot to spot where I thought we should have turned off, found the gap and plunged in. A voice, disembodied, coming from the shadow of a truck, answered my query and told us we were at Sidi Omar, where 4th Ind. Div. were located.

Joined balance of the convoy and were told there would be a two-hour rest before pushing on. Spent this time trying to plug a leaking radiator, extricate a bumper from beneath the front mudguard, and other odds and ends.

On again, cold, hungry, eyes closed up with dust and mouth full of grit. Then—another blow-out on No. 2 truck. It was useless to attempt to repair it in the dark and so lose the convoy again, so off-loaded most of the kit on to my car and the truck with the leaky radiator. Pushed on. Caught convoy but (why ? I do not really know except that my miserly soul couldn't bear to leave the punctured truck behind) I decided against continuing. Stopped, waited for first light.

It was deathly cold. There were the hulks of knocked-out tanks and burned vehicles around us, a minefield on either side of the narrow path, and two lonely Royal Sussex sentries hissing into their cold hands to warm them.

They had a terrific battle for this place.

It is actually Sidi Omar Nuovo, the most northerly of the three Omars—Libyan, Sidi and Sidi Nuovo—and the other two are held by Boche and Wops. Not more than 5 kilometres separates any Omar from the other.

As soon as the edge of the world turned grey, trudged off to find the punctured truck, the other vehicles crawling along behind me. Snatches of a poem by A. E. Housman beat time with my slow feet—

" Yonder see the morning blink

[Left, right, left, right, left, right ; wish they'd put a few more notices up in this bloody minefield ; left, right.]

> Let me lie abed and rest :
> Ten thousand times I've done my best,
> And all's to do again."

Found the truck. A few gunners and Royal Sussex people stared at us from beneath woollen hats and socks tied round their heads.

Changed the wheel and was about to set off to find Div. when shelling began and lasted 35 minutes. A slit-trench would have been a nice thing. My car hit three times by shell splinters but no real damage done and none of my chickens hurt.

Contacted Div. H.Q. at 08.15 hrs. At 09.30 hrs. Sam was cooking breakfast, Bayliss and Noble were trying to mend the busted radiator—all between ten-minute bursts of shellfire from three different directions.

On the other side of the wire—the Egyptian side—could see a fair amount of our M.T. moving down towards Scheferzen.

The day went on interminably ; shelling pretty severe. In the afternoon there were two violent tank attacks upon us. The first one came in on a bearing of about 120 degrees as I stood talking to the Divisional Commander. The dust from shellbursts and scurrying tanks made it almost impossible to follow the battle, but through the glasses I saw the Boche retired over the rim of a hill.

Went back to my trucks then to organise things a bit,

should we have a chance to poop off; immediately there was another tank charge launched by 38 Mk. III's. They came in (at a shallow angle and roughly 600 yds. away from us) in echelon, looking very fierce and warlike, firing like blazes and clearly concentrating on the gun positions holding the entrance to our position.

Black beasts of things, they looked : squat and ugly. Thought our people were never going to fire. They let them come on in bounds, and then at 500 yds. range they cracked into them. Oh God ! it was terrific stuff. Fairly belched shells. I stood on top of the car, glasses trained on the battle, giving (I'm told, though I do not recall it) a running commentary containing more bad language than an officer strictly should use.

Twice the Boche charged, used some dead ground to re-form, and charged again. The gunners never wavered in the least. They kept walloping the stuff over. After 15 minutes, the Boche hauled off and beat it in the direction of Sidi Omar—in the dip behind our main minefield. I saw 21 of them go. The others were dotted about, smoking or just stopped and still.

Then our bombers and flocks of fighters appeared. They must have got wind of the scrap, I should think. The bombers dropped masses of stuff from high level and then the fighters zoomed down on the wretched Boche and smartened him no end, one imagined— couldn't see for the dip, of course. But there was a nice lot of black smoke around.

Let Bayliss and Noble take one of my trucks out to photograph the knocked-out tanks. They returned with documents and maps taken from one, which I took to the General's G.1. Might be some useful stuff among them.

Almost at last light saw the General again. He was rubbing his thin, mittened hands and said the gunners have knocked out 16 Boche tanks in all to-day and the R.E. people are now fondly burning them. The gunners lost four pieces, knocked out, and had a good few casualties; also a Coy. of Rajputana Rifles was over-run and there is no news of them yet.

I have 30 gallons of water left (nine people to cater for) and 26 gallons of petrol (scrounged) in Boche containers which I collected during the flap back yesterday.

To bed now, feeling somewhat worn, I must say; the sight of our people doing their stuff puts a song in my heart, though.

26 Nov. 41.   10.00 HRS.   *At Sidi Omar Nuovo*

Slept well until 04.30 hrs. when m.g. fire to South-West woke me. Then some very low-flying aircraft came over, dropped flares with horrible persistence and bombed us like the dickens. They cleared off as the first breath of dawn came sidling over the horizon.

At sun-up our Hurricanes came over to bomb and machine-gun the blokes down the road (at Sidi Omar—mostly Wops with a Boche stiffening, I hear) while we had a not-too-bad shelling. It is almost impossible to describe the layout of things here, though it is perfectly clear on a map. But it is such that we are shelled from three sides regularly. A long line of Wop prisoners filed in a few minutes ago. 'Struth! what a measly crowd they do look, though I suppose no one looks his best as a P.O.W.

LATER (Watch has stopped)

Contacted Bde. H.Q., Infy. Bde., of this Div. and my favourite Brigadier. Also Indian P.R. and Quentin Reynolds. Did not know the blighters were here—so deep is their most splendid trench (a Wop effort, of course).

A good many Italian and Boche prisoners rolling in.

Bayliss and Noble went out to their tank again, and behold ! the R.E.'s had burned it out during the night and three Wops were hiding inside for warmth and shelter from their dear Axis partners. They complained bitterly about hard conditions and much shelling ; pathetic people : one really has little time for them.

The day ended on a note that makes me horribly depressed. One of the drivers put my own truck into a gigantic slit-trench. I simply dare not look at it.

27 Nov. 41   *At Sidi Omar Nuovo*

Very heavy packet of gunfire and much m.g. fire began just before dawn. Three Coys. of our troops went in to winkle a few people out from Libyan Omar. They got a good haul.

Worked all morning with aid of a L.A.D. Coy. (old Jarabub friends, of whom there are a great many here) and got my truck out. It looks horribly mangled but still runs. The Indians are working on it.

A food and water convoy came in during the night from Conference Cairn.

During the afternoon nine Boche Mk. III's came alongside the minefield, working towards the gun positions.

Then, for some reason, they sat there looking very puzzled and apparently wondering quite what to do. Our guns, by plan, did not open fire at them. It was the oddest sight. There were they and here were we, and nothing happened until some gunner got impatient and bunged over a trial 6-inch shell. At which the Boche turned away while all the other guns, chagrined at seeing them go, let fly with the dickens of a noise. They claim a hit, which in this case meant a certain tank, because they aren't so good with 6-inch shells tickling them up.

Great news then. My truck will be all right and running in a couple of days.

And greater news still; much greater. A cipher message came in saying that we had occupied Sidi Rezegh again and that Tobruk had linked up once more.

Meantime, the Boche is doing all he can to hammer the resistance out of us here and elsewhere and stop us re-forming. He sent a large column—tanks, guns and much M.T.—along the Trigh Capuzzo yesterday. It went into Bardia (the area up there is being held by New Zealanders), came out again, swept down almost due South, wiped up the N.Z. Bde. H.Q. at Sidi Azeiz, now cracking into the N.Z. people at Fort Capuzzo, 20 km. N.E. of us along the frontier.

I feel that we simply must hang on here, and that probably this part of the world may prove to be absolutely vital for our success.

28 Nov. 41 *At Sidi Omar Nuovo*

Got my truck back to-day and scrounged a sun-compass as make-weight. Very important—a message says that the Boche has ordered his armoured raiding forces to withdraw in a N.-Westerly direction. This will relieve the attacks on our L. of C. at this end and means that he is really worried about himself all over again.

We have beaten his thrust at our heart; that much is certain. Now he is turning back to re-fight the Sidi Rezegh battle, I suppose. We have done awfully well to re-form quickly enough to make him do this.

A New Zealander came into the camp looking a bit the worse for wear. The Sidi Azeiz shindy was pretty bad, it seems, but we held on at Fort Capuzzo all right.

Not a great deal of news coming in here, though, apart from the major thing about the Boche clearing off. Am thinking of busting out to make 8th Army H.Q. to-morrow; at the moment the people here seem to think we might get wiped up—some odds and ends still sculling around between here and Maddalena ; also, our own troops out there are a bit quick on the trigger, especially as the Boche have been using some of our captured vehicles to snoop up and surprise isolated parties.

Fair amount of air activity and some shelling—mostly our own—and it seems that at least some of the enemy artillery has cleared off.

My good friends gave me eight gallons of water ; this means an extra cup of tea this evening for everyone and (if I'm in the same benevolent mood by to-morrow) a wash all round, which will be the first for 11 days. I cancelled the order about shaving each day when we got here, so we all have beards of a sort. Best of all is the General's effort—a real tiger.

Just as night was falling, 16 socking great I-tanks rumbled into camp, my Tanks captain pal leading them rather like a proud hen parading her first brood of gangling, ugly chickens. My drivers stood by and cheered them, and Sam, Matt and Alaric looked at them with a cheery, if speculative, eye.

29 Nov. 41   *Nr. Maddalena with 8th Army H.Q.*

A huge cup of strong coffee (using our buckshee water) all round, a filling of petrol containers, testing of tyres, route-setting and general tidying-up, and we were ready to move from Omar Nuovo. Course 140 deg. to Conference Cairn, thence 200 deg. to Army—46 m.

Said good-bye and thanks a lot to the Brig., B.M. Peter Hughes (whose beard is now surely the most wonderful thing in the desert), and to the Staff Captain, whose beaming face has made me ashamed of any fleeting moments of depression or weariness.

I was given despatches and dispositions for Army H.Q. and we sailed out, through the minefield, past the gunners, past nine burned-out Boche tanks, over the hill and onwards.

Arrived here on a good bearing—slap in the centre of the camp, which *always* makes me childishly proud—and passed over my stuff to Army Ops., who, incidentally, seemed to think I might have presented a less grubby appearance and who stared at my back-pad (a rubber cushion I use strapped to the small of my back to soften the jolting when I'm up on the bridge navigating) as if it was a clear case of unauthorised equipment.

Saw the C.O. and learned, with astonishment, that we had been reported missing, believed captured. Hope they didn't tell my Shena that, dammit.

Seems that a lot of the South African journalists are in the bag also, Eddie Ward, *B.B.C.*, my pal Harold Denny, *New York Times*, who at one time was going to join my party, and Godfrey Anderson of *U.P.* Do not know yet where they were captured. A black shame, for they were all very decent people, especially old Denny, who never forgot a dry stew I made him in the last campaign.

All the other conducting officers and parties had had their share of adventures. John Brooke, who shares my tent in the ordinary way of business and burns my pyjamas as a hobby—the hound—got shot up going through a Boche camp in error.

Organised a terrific hot wash and shave for everyone and am now about to join John Brooke in a whisky; in fact, several whiskies, if he has them.

30 Nov. 41 *Nr. Maddalena with 8th Army*

A day of rest—almost, anyhow. Heard that one of our trucks had blown itself up in a minefield and went seeking it in the afternoon with John Brooke. Failed, but did get location of the minefield, roughly, so intend to go there again to-morrow. The big lure is water and

some grub aboard the thing ; also, maybe, some tyres—
and some booze.

General picture of the war is extremely hard to come
by. Most of the Boche seem now to have retired to the
Sidi Rezegh area, where tank battles are in progress.
They hold also at El Adem and El Gubbi.

The R.A.F. seem to have done well, their score being
around 170 at the moment, I believe. Saw Richard
Capell of the *Daily Telegraph*, an old campaigning friend
who tells *any* story more wittily than Oscar Wilde. He
excelled himself with recounting his adventures when a
female war correspondent put in an appearance in the
desert.

1 DEC. 41   *Nr. Maddalena with 8th Army*

Spent most of the day in the minefield salving the
truck. John Brooke and I divided the spoils—a good
haul of water, petrol, food, tyres, etc.

The fabled whisky, alleged to be on the truck, could
not be found, alas !

Had a cable from my Shena wishing me a happy birth-
day, and realised with a jolt that I was 34 last Sept. 22.

Sam Brewer flew back to Cairo yesterday and Richard
Mowrer, *Chicago Daily News*, joins my party in his place ;
am off to-morrow, not caring over-much to be in the
somewhat rarefied atmosphere of these high places and
also wanting to get back to the real battle. Sorry to lose
Sam, who has been a great help in keeping the log and
checking bearings.

2 DEC. 41   *Sidi Omar Nuovo*

A fearfully cold, grey day. Heavy wind and great
booming gusts of rain that made navigation difficult and
soaked me to the skin up on the bridge. Spent most of

the morning reorganising stores, kit, checking over the vehicles, which seem to be in reasonable fettle despite the grim treatment since the campaign began.

Fred Salusbury, of the *Daily Herald*, joined my party with an extra car at the last moment.

An hour at Army Ops. marking the map for delivery to the General and then off. Devilish bad journey, but made it to find we had captured Libyan Omar, rooting out 400 Boche prisoners and flocks of Wops. The General is expecting to be relieved by 2nd South African Div. soon and to push on forward. Where he goes, I go. This man is a great general, and most kindly withal.

The Boche Panzer has had another crack at us and has broken the Tobruk corridor again, according to latest advice, after the most sanguinary fighting.

This is a set-back. Our own armour is re-forming and we still claim numerical superiority. One has to realise that the Boche tanks—especially the Mk. III with 105 mm. gun—have an edge on most of ours, and that we have to beat him by tactics and sheer good fighting. We shall do it all right ; no doubt of *that* ; our tank people are simply terrific, and a tatty old infantryman like myself raises the largest size hat to them.

The scrap here for Libyan Omar was a good one ; sorry I missed it. My ears are flapping at a rumour that there is some Wop bottled mineral water knocking around, so I have turned my scrounger-in-chief loose with the instructions to seek it out.

3 DEC. 41   *With 30th Corps South of Trigh el Abd*

Planned to go up the wire to Sollum and see the form there, when I heard that the Boche and Wops were massing at El Adem—South of Tobruk—with the Panzers on their left, at Sidi Rezegh (estimated 100 tanks), and that we plan a dawn attack to-morrow with

11th Hussars, Guards Brigade, 11th Indian Inf. Brigade and an Armoured Brigade.

This looked good. So off to 30th Corps. A long chase and some very tricky navigation.

Came through masses of our tanks moving up for the battle, the crews as cheery as crickets and making dirty cracks about my back-pad, bless them.

At Corps the information was confirmed. Then, at the last moment, the whole plan was washed out. Do not yet know what the form is.

4 DEC. 41   *With 7th Armd. Div. North of Trigh el Abd*

Oh ! but it is deathly cold in these parts. We make a little petrol fire in the sand and feed it with brushwood to thaw out until the sun warms up. All night could hear tanks and M.T. moving up under a brilliant full moon ; there was also some banging about—fairly small calibre, I should think. I have solved the problem of keeping warm in my sleeping-bag. I simply do not take off *any* clothes—boots excepted—put on a balaclava, and then finish off by wrapping a woollen scarf about on head and neck. The truck is so placed as to keep off the worst of the wind.

I have just my nose and mouth exposed, and Matt, who is always last into bed, shoves a cigarette between my lips before he wraps up ; then I have to keep my head over the side of the camp-bed for fear of setting myself alight, my arms and hands being too tightly inside the sleeping-bag to be of any use. We usually jaw for 15 minutes or so, mostly about books and plays and posts and home and hot baths.

Sam always has something interesting to tell about Albania or Greece, where the campaign was very sticky indeed, and with him I like talking mechanics. Alaric does not talk much but occasionally, when pressed, sings a grand little song about a lunatic asylum.

But by half-past seven everyone is asleep and we do not wake until dawn ; that is, unless there is a lot of noise or the eternal Boche leaguer lights flaming up into the night. They are as bad as the Chinese for letting off lights ; they simply love them, and keep good citizens of the desert from sleeping thereby, curse them !

It turned out during the morning that last night's big battle was put off in favour of a smaller action over at El Gubbi in which the 11th Ind. Infantry Bde. and the 4th A.B. took part.

Have just remembered that, while at Army H.Q., I saw the new Army Commander, Major-General Ritchie, who has taken General Cunningham's place. He came into the Ops. tent while I was there—huge, handsome man, most extraordinarily smartly turned out and fairly oozing energy and vigour.

Pushed off to 7th Armd. Div. Adv. H.Q., who said that the battle had produced a couple of hundred prisoners and that we had knocked out 16 tanks—Wops. Meantime the Boche is reported to be at his old tricks again and is humming along the Trigh Capuzzo in an easterly direction with a strong bunch of tanks, guns and M.E.T. The 11th Hussars and a strong column are engaging them all the time. No one here seems unduly worried about this Boche effort, though I must say that I do not like the smell of it.

We go into close leaguer with 7th A.D. to-night, with a good, healthy wad of tanks around us. This leaguer idea is surely a throw-back to the oldest sort of warfare. Everyone withdraws into a tight bunch—the soft transport in the centre and the armoured stuff and guards on the perimeter. Do I not remember the Romans doing this ?

5 DEC. 41   *With 30th Corps H.Q.*

It gets colder. But sun-up was bright and cheerful.

The 11th Ind. Infantry Bde. is still in action at El Gubbi —rather North and West of it—and the S.A. Armd. Car chaps have done a wonderful job of work. They snooped round the back of the enemy and got at his main food, oil and ammunition dumps, also a couple of grounded planes. They sent the whole ruddy lot up in flames, and from here we can see a great column of smoke climbing lazily up into the blue. The dump had 50,000 gals. of petrol, 10,000 gals. of fuel oil, a hell of a lot of food. I'll bet this has shaken them.

The General has been relieved at the Omars and is bringing the 4th Ind. Div. around in a great sweep so as to face the enemy here. This is a daring move. My talc looks grim to-night—as it has done in the past. Rommel has seen our threat to his right flank, based on El Gubbi, and his recce. planes have obviously blown the gaff about the Indians moving. So he is massing troops and armour to meet us. He holds Sidi Rezegh, is strong at El Adem, and from there his line runs due South to El Gubbi. Rather the shape of a figure seven written backwards. At the same time he has this column of his still sculling around the Trigh Capuzzo eastwards, but being harried now by two of our columns. And to create further diversion and try to unsettle us, he has a column of guns, armd. cars and lorried infantry striking down towards the Trigh el Abd behind us.

Maybe he hopes this last column will be able to interfere ; in that case he is in for a pretty good thick ear.

I go to bed to-night very, very tired and struggling with a bout of worry over the M.T. I have checked every damned thing we have, but am having bad luck with punctures again. The water situation is quite reasonable on the face of it, but I am never satisfied that I have enough and hoard the stuff like gold. Strictly I should go back for a refit, I suppose, but I'm blowed if I will. Accidents barred, we can feed and water ourselves for another 11 days, I reckon, and I shall try to do this as, so far as I know, mine is the only party in the field at the moment.

6 DEC. 41 *With 30th Corps*

At 11.00 hrs. saw the General, and the picture he drew was brief and heartening. He is an enormously equable man, wears his hat with a Beatty slant, and talks in the gentle, soothing way one does when standing in front of a roaring fire watching the butler pour out the port.

Well then, the Boche and Wops made two terrific moonlight attacks on the 11th Ind. Infantry Bde. last night just as they were preparing to withdraw through the Gds. Bde. Both attacks were severe and a lot of casualties on both sides. But the Indians held them and the Gds. to-day take over that flank to give them respite. Rommel is still piling up troops and guns along the El Adem-El Gubbi line. What remains of the Ariete is engaging the 4th A.B. on the East of this line, while further to the North of this shindy the recce. planes report the remnants of Rommel's Armoured Divs.—15th and 21st Panzer Regts. We have bowled over another 15 of the Ariete machines, and I suppose Rommel wants to lure us further on so that he can counter-attack our armour while it is still smartening the Wops. I do not see us falling for that one, I must say.

The General seemed confident that we are turning the scales and regaining the superiority we had before the first big Boche counter-attack, which so nearly snookered us (by " us," I mean my party). He specially mentioned the South African Armd. Cars, whom he calls his " mosquitoes " and who are all the time worrying away at the enemy's flanks and his L. of C. Incidentally, in addition to all the food, petrol and so on the S.A. chaps got, they also burned out a lot of M.T.

Ashwood of *Movietone* and Lt. Vanderson, Official War

Photographer, last seen at Sidi Omar, turned up and told of finding some of the Italian bottled water which I sent Downs to scrounge. He was unsuccessful, so am passing him across to Vanderson for tuition.

18.00 HRS.

Had intended to move across to 4th Ind. Div. now in position 7 m. away when great news arrived. General movement of the enemy *westwards*! They're beating it. The move of bringing round the 4th Ind. Div. is responsible for this, I'll bet anything. Their Trigh Capuzzo column has turned tail, having got completely fed up with being prodded about, and I do not wonder at it. The column reported to be moving round the back of us also has cleared off. It seems most probable that there is a general withdrawal by the enemy, but he is putting up a strong rearguard action. Sidi Rezegh is reported ours again, and Tobruk coming out in style. Hooray! I wonder what has happened to all my friends in the 4th Tank Regt.—Ben Cole and Jim Kendall, especially. They were in Tobruk.

During the afternoon saw a most charming Brigadier R.E.—a New Zealander—who told of bowling up to Sidi Rezegh some days back and somehow getting ahead of our own troops. Some sportsman opened up on his car with a machine-gun, sending three rounds slick through the windscreen. The Brigadier and his companions— two of them—stopped, hopped out and ran for it. The bullets fairly hummed around them, and one actually took off a fly-button from the Brigadier's trousers.

Sam and Matt and Alaric, my driver and myself—we all went pale at this recital. He said, " I'm not kidding. Look ! " and sure enough there was a neat tear and one button missing. My driver seemed more profoundly moved than any others of us, for an hour later he said, with a very serious face, " War is awful, ain't it ? "

Incidentally, the Brigadier got his car back, plugged the holes up and tied other bits on with string. In the scrap which followed after he'd been shot at, both sides used the car as cover, so it was a pretty sight.

7 DEC. 41   *At Bir Duedar with 7th Bde. 4th Ind. Div.*

There is the devil of a lot of shuffling around to-day, and we are pressing the Boche hard and not giving him much of a chance to settle in anywhere too comfortably. The armoured cars keep at his flanks all the time; the R.A.F. is simply magnificent and sends over wave after wave of fighters and bombers; if they are doing such here, what are they doing to his L. of C., I wonder. Everyone agrees that at no time, not even during the time when we pedalled back and must have presented great targets, has the Luftwaffe been really active and troublesome; of course, they *have* done some bombing— quite a bit with Stukas—but I have failed to see any evidence of it having marked effect. In other sectors further North it may be different; but I doubt it.

Fred Bayliss, whom we left at Army H.Q. and who dodged down to Cairo for a new truck, came into camp as we were preparing to leave 30th Corps and come on here. Bless him, he brought lots and lots of tinned foodstuffs, a little whisky, and—best of all—cigarettes. He seems to think he is in our debt for watering and feeding him at the Omars, which is absurd.

The enemy line now is much shortened. He seems to have got most of his stuff away from the area East of Sidi Rezegh, including the remnants of the Bologna Div., which suffered very heavy casualties during the fighting on the East of the Tobruk perimeter. Now he holds from El Adem to El Gubbi, and our recce. planes report steady movement of his transport towards the West.

It is good to be back among these people again. They

gave us a most kind welcome. Went right forward to a Field Bty. R.A. just short of El Gubbi and rather East of it. The Brigadier R.A. says his people have now *destroyed* at least 25 Boche tanks and smartened up goodness knows how many more. There should be a special heaven for gunners.

Had rather a spread for dinner, Fred Bayliss actually making some custard—a most magnificent effort—to follow the stew.

8 Dec. 41   *With 7th Bde. 4th Ind. Div. at Belchonfuss*

It was damnably cold during the night, but there was no dew to soak the fleabags and make them look like the bedraggled hem of Calamity's petticoat ; and the nip of whisky before going to bed was superb, of course.

Up early intending, if the El Adem–El Gubbi line looked like holding for any length of time, to go to Tobruk, then along the Trigh Capuzzo to Bardia, Sollum, Sidi Omar, and finally Army H.Q.

But the line has not held. Overnight the blighters had departed from El Gubbi, our patrols reported, so orders were immediately given for the Bde. to move. We came on here and intend to sweep on and lambast the Boche while he is running. But at the moment we are rather stuck, because a large tank battle is reported ahead of us.

I went forward this afternoon among a perfect welter of knocked-out and burned-out Boche and Italian tanks (also three of ours) and masses of M.T. and motor-cycle combinations and got to El Gubbi. Ground very badly cut up with trenches and defence works ; three very tatty-looking shacks much knocked about by shelling ; a large signpost pointing the tracks to Bardia, Gazala, etc., and a huge compass-face made of stone and let into the ground ; centuries-old track junction, this place ; the bir (water cistern) there had been in use recently and our water engineers were already on the job testing it and seeing if their complicated-looking effort machines could do anything about it. Struck me as being a good smooth for these chaps to be on the job before even the advancing troops had settled in. Scrounged round for an hour or so and collared some useful tools and things.

Just before going up to El Gubbi, we were machine-gunned by 10 Me. 109's.   They killed a few people, including one chap who was just getting out of his truck to hop into a slit-trench ; bad luck. The Brig. had two bullets through the back of his staff car but was not hurt. The Germans are much better at machine-gunning than the Italians and really do put a bit of guts into it. Can't say that I care over-much for it.

Just as the petal dust of twilight was falling we moved forward and then came to the very rough and tumbled ground I had encountered earlier. Since it would have been very dangerous to have negotiated this in darkness, the Bde. stopped and leaguered for the night.

Now it is past time for bed, and most people's minds are in a whirl because we have just heard on the radio that the Japs have attacked the States and smartened up quite a bit of their fleet. The Americans with me seem pleased and, maybe, relieved that at last they are really in the war as combatants. Mowrer thinks he ought to get back to Cairo and report to his Embassy because he is on the U.S. Naval Reserve ; the others have similar ideas. Reminds me so much of Sept. 1939 at home, when Mike Killanin rang me at the office and said to be on parade that night and that my mobilisation papers had been sent round to the flat.

9 DEC. 41.   09.00 HRS.   *Halted on way to El Adem*
We have stopped briefly to make a cup of tea. There

I woke at 03.00 hrs. with the moon shining very brightly on my face.

And there was a bird chirruping in the strangest manner—two notes, a low and then a high one, saying *"Audrey! Audrey!"*

At 05.30 we were off on a course slightly North of West, muffled to the ears and very chilly. Now, over to our left, there is a steady roar of moving tanks. Sometimes the wind brings the odd cough of their engines and identifies them to me as American, so I suppose it is part of Armoured Bde. sculling about. About here there has been some very heavy fighting. Lots of dead Boches but few Wops. Many knocked-out tanks (including one of our cruisers, burned out). There are two large Italian hospital tents over to the right: I wish I had the time to go across and see if any of our people are there and needing anything. From the look of the mess which enemy M.T. is in about these parts, I should think the R.A.F. caught them napping and bombed the lights out of them.

15.30 HRS.   *At El Adem Aerodrome*

Well, we are here at last and the Boche is still moving back. The General has just come over to say things are going very well and that we shall stay the night here and push on due West after the enemy to-morrow. Nothing much here except melancholy wrecks of Italian and some German machines—some of them this campaign's and some last year's. All the aerodrome buildings seem to be shattered to hell. A couple of Boche were found hiding in a hole in the ground just as we arrived; they got up just in time to get their hands in the air and looked for all the world like a couple of scarecrows.

On the way here, we were halted for a couple of hours

and some terrific air battles went on overhead; three Boche down and one of ours.

I took a couple of Wops (from the Ariete Div.) back to Armd. Div. in my truck and as a result feel that the thing should be fumigated; they were the dirtiest creatures I've seen for years and simply stank.

Through the glass I can see great lines of our M.T. moving West along the El Adem–Acroma road; lots of guns and stuff, also some I-tanks.

Have just counted nearly 60 of our fighters and 32 bombers going off to give the Boche a sundowner. The sky seemed full of planes and I should think some of the old hands in Tobruk, looking at them, must have rubbed their eyes.

This night, in consideration of our advance, I put on my red silk pyjamas though it is going to be deathly cold, and I am going to curse such melodramatic rashness. Still, one must make a gesture sometimes.

10 DEC. 41   *Tobruk*

Well, I did my best to keep out of this place and stay with our advancing troops, but luck was against me. Early this morning the Brig. said would I like to go with him on his recce. towards Acroma, where the Bde. was ordered to move. Jumped at the chance, of course, and then found that overnight the evil sprites had got at my transport.

The starter motor on my own truck refused to function, and the Humber saloon coughed and spluttered and sent up clouds of foul smoke. So I couldn't go with the Brigadier or chance moving forward. It meant coming in here for repairs.

It was disappointing. The General was in cracking form, and hearing that I'd slept in silk pyjamas overnight and seeing me freshly shaved, said I was a ·bloody

Sybarite and a disgrace to his Army ! He is such a grand person.

Got my truck to start by towing it and then jogged into Tobruk in a violent rainstorm. Found here many old friends and colleagues, all of them looking rather tired, and heard with deep sorrow that Jim Kendall, my special pal in 4th Tank Regt., was killed some days ago in the break-out towards Sidi Rezegh after putting up a wonderful show.

In the severe fighting up in this sector, great deeds were done and all evening I sat listening to stories of them. There were some tigerish battles.

To-night I sleep in a tent.

11 DEC. 41   *On Axis-Strasse nr. Acroma*

It took so long to get away from Tobruk that it was very late when we contacted the New Zealand Bde. (with new H.Q. staff) at Acroma. Ind. Div. were here until midday, but they have pushed on after the Boche on the left flank. The devil of a day : high winds and severe dust storms. Met up with a Bn. of the King's Own who were occupying the *ridotti* at Acroma. This Bn., Geoffrey Keating tells me, carried out a model operation with the Tks. in the Tobruk break-out ; they attacked and captured " Butch," a strong-point of great importance, in great style and with small casualties.

A good deal of enemy equipment lying around here, including some very large guns of the " Bardia Bill " type.

The general form at the moment is that the New Zealanders are to advance along the line of the main coast road which leads to Gazala with one Bn., and along the top of the escarpment on a parallel course with their other two Bns. The Ind. Div. are on their left in this advance, and Army Tank Bde. is giving them armoured support.

The enemy is still reported to be withdrawing along the coast road in the direction of Derna, but there is some opposition expected forward of Gazala and, probably, quite a strong rearguard action to be dealt with actually at Gazala. There are two landing grounds there which are of great importance to us now for fighter support, and although the Boche cannot use them himself now, we being too close on his tail, he'll undoubtedly try to keep us off them as long as possible.

Our Armoured Bde. intends to go round left of the 4th Ind. Div. and make a wide sweep up and behind the enemy to a place called Eleba. They will need to watch Mekili also, I imagine.

To-night we hide up in some old Italian gun positions to get out of the fierce wind. Geoffrey Keating, who joined the Army with me and is now an official War Office Photographer, stays the night with us and joins in my stew with gusto.

12 DEC. 41   15 *m. West of Acroma*

Forward, and contacted Army Tank Bde., from whom we heard something of the great tank battles at Ed Duda during the Tobruk break-out. Saw also Bon Cole, old friend with Jim Kendall, who has his majority—most deservedly. He achieved the almost impossible feat of putting all his tanks into battle as runners on the great day ; one knows that in 99 per cent. of cases *some* have to be left out because of this or that good reason.

Immediately forward of us, the K.D.G.'s have just been Stuka'd and the N.Z. people on our right seem to be getting stick. Our turn next.

LATER

I want to get on over to the Ind. Div., but am not

precise as to their location. The New Zealanders, now moving forward on our left (that is, the two Bns. which are to go along the top of the escarpment), had a grand battle last evening. Their Maori Bn. ran on to a very strong Italian position thick with artillery and many anti-tank guns. By some superb manœuvring and really magnificent use of ground, they wiped out the entire force and captured 14 guns, 25 anti-tank guns, and endless other bits and pieces. They so timed their attack that they were able to go in with the bayonet just at the last. Round about where they are now, there is a main track (not marked on the map) which leads along the escarpment and to Gazala, and the air recces. show that there is a good deal of abandoned and knocked-out traffic on this track, so I suppose the fierceness of the Maoris' attack must have panicked them.

It seems likely that this particular party of Wops, anyhow, were surprised by the speed of our advance and that their supporting troops on right and left failed to help them out ; otherwise how would such a strong force be left completely isolated like that ?

My party agrees that it might be a good thing to delay going out to the left flank in search of the Indians and stay with either the tanks or with the New Zealanders. Fred Salusbury of the *Daily Herald* went back to Tobruk to-day with the Humber and intends to rejoin us later. Fred Bayliss went off in search of an A.B. and we probably shall not see him for a time now. So my party is reduced to two—Matt Halton and Alaric Jacob—good fellows who have not once grumbled at rather trying times, restrictions on water, very plain food and so on, and who never buck at going into a good battle. Their conduct, and that of my three drivers, has been first-rate all through. Matt is now keeping the log, and both he and Alaric buckle-to and give a hand with the cooking (which I like doing myself) and making camp, etc.

13 DEC. 41   *8 m. South of Gazala*

Moved off at 07.30 hrs. and passed through the place where the Maoris settled the Wops. Guns and equipment everywhere. It must have been a party, and the more one saw of the strength of the position—the ground here is very broken and quite unlike that further back, where it is mostly flat or very gently undulating—the more one admired the Maoris for their skill and resolution.

We constantly came upon overturned Italian lorries, most of them burned out and with their dead lying grotesquely in heaps beside them. And the Bersaglieri had passed that way. Dozens of their motor-cycles, smashed and shattered by hard going and machine-gunning, were about ; and their topees, bearing a pluck of green cock's feathers, sat dismally about on the track, squashed and shapeless. Very rarely had the retreating Italians had time to bury their dead ; occasionally they had laid a chap out and crossed his hands over his chest, but not often. We couldn't stop to do anything about it and had to leave it to B Echelon people coming along in our wake.

Caught up with N.Z. Bde. H.Q. and learned from the Maori I.O. that their Bn., supported by I-tanks, had made grand progress along the road and had secured the two landing grounds. Their other two Bns. were hammering away forward and encountering stiff opposition. Shelling about these parts is quite considerable, and there is a lot of air activity on both sides. The 23rd Bn. patrols recaptured some Indians who had been taken prisoner earlier in the battle. They also found, in a wadi just in rear of where we are at the moment, a mass of transport, all in good condition, and quite a few guns.

We were talking to a chap, and he said had we heard about some Italian prisoners shooting a Boche who was captured with them. One has to be very careful and

sure of these stories, so we checked up immediately with
the I.O. and he verified it and showed us the report on
the matter.   Apparently ten Wops and one Boche were
collared during some patrolling by the Bn., and as they
were being rounded up, one of the Wops whipped out
his automatic and shot the Boche in the back.

As evening fell darkly and sombrely, with many heavy
clouds making the air cold and damp, some Tanks
rumbled through and out to our left flank and were followed by a Battery of 25-pounders.   Very soon there was
a lot of banging about and now, all along the line, there
is heavy gunfire, while far away—at least 10 miles, I
should think—there seems to be the whale of a battle
going on : this will be Ind. Div. for a ducat ; we must
get over to them as soon as possible ; they are a bit South
of West of this position.

There is no news of Armd. Bde., but we hear that the
Polish Brigade, or part of it, is coming forward from the
Tobruk area.   Hope they reach us in time, before the
position gives way ; they must be simply dying to get
their hands on some Boche and one would hate them to
be disappointed.

14 Dec. 41   *With 13th Corps*

All through the night there was gunfire and, immediately forward of us, quite a bit of m.g. fire.   Someone
suggested, just before we went to bed, that it might be
a good idea not to put up the camp-beds but to sleep
just in the bed-rolls, so that if we had to breeze suddenly
we could do so with the least delay.   There could be no
criticism of such an eminently and obviously sensible
notion, but, having stuck to the principle of putting up
the beds at all times, I did not care to depart from it.
There is quite a bit of morale-strengthening to be
obtained from sleeping in forward areas precisely as one

would sleep back at base. Also, I think that if one really had to hop out of a position in a hurry there would not, in any case, be time to worry about beds or bedding. That is why I insist (much to the drivers' disgust) on re-loading practically everything we use after our evening meal; I know it is a fag and a bore, but it would be an even greater bore to lose the stuff. You simply cannot play about with the desert in our circumstances. We must be, at all times, completely self-contained and not have to throw ourselves on the mercy of the chaps who are actually pressing the triggers.

Army Tank Bde. moved off at 08.00 hrs., having had a pleasing little scrap last evening and helped the New Zealanders snaffle quite a few Wops who were drifting in in droves as we left.

They are really grand people, these New Zealanders; they just hate sitting around and have the offensive spirit *in excelsis*. I have always been taught that night attacks are the best, most other things being equal; and they believe in this implicitly. Their last night's operation—with a limited objective—was most successful.

We fetched up with 4th Ind. Div. H.Q., who, it turned out, were roughly 12 miles S.W. of us. They have been having a very sticky time indeed, and all look a trifle worn but in great heart. The Indian Bdes. have been fighting like tigers. First the Boche attacked the 7th Bde. with (estimated) 40–50 tanks. Again those wonderful gunners waited, then gripped the tanks by the throat and throttled them. Guns they have lost—yes; but the tank attack failed. It was beaten. Thrashed and mangled. They left more than a dozen tanks on the field. Oh, I wish we had been there.

The Stukas have been concentrating on this Div., but they are getting more than they give. When they attack, everyone settles himself in a slit-trench—except the A.A. people, of course—and looses off any weapon that comes to hand. The variety of bangs has to be heard to be believed.

Matt Halton and Alaric Jacob were anxious to flash back to Army H.Q. and collect any cables and instructions and to get a broader picture of the offensive, so I set a course right away, it being latish, which took us through 13th Corps.

There we ran into Fred Salusbury, *Daily Herald*, back with the Humber and about to set off and look for us. He had masses of mail for me from my 9-months-old son, whom I have yet to see ; and some handkerchiefs— most welcome. The C.O. sent some tinned food and cigarettes.

Corps were able to give us a good picture, and as Fred had just left Army and had all the news, there was no need to go there. Decided to stay the rest of the day and push forward again to-morrow.

Just before arriving here we ran into the Polish Brigade, who simply could not get forward quick enough —grand chaps.

NOTE ON M.T.

Ford Saloon

    Mileage : as logged.   5006.1 m.

    Chassis : Fine crack developing in forward cross-member as result of crash in slit-trench at Sidi Omar.

    Springs : Good.

    Tyres :   One rear discarded ; walls burst and under-size fitted in its place. Now without spare, although have one patched inner-tube.

    Starter : Developed fault which could not be traced. New battery was fitted in Tobruk but same

Note on M.T.—*continued.*

trouble recurred. Fault was finally traced to control-box, which had been wired in slipshod manner.

General : Minor damage sustained to windscreen and body by shell splinters. Radiator grill broken. Rear bumper missing. Off-side front and both rear wings badly dented. Sump needs draining and differential topping.

Ford 10-cwt.

Mileage : as logged. 5115.7.

Chassis : Needs greasing and oiling. Exhaust pipe expansion chamber punctured by stones.

Springs : Fair ; front one bedding down a little.

Tyres : Good but showing wear on rear and off-side front. One (patched) spare available.

Battery : Needs draining and new distilled water.

General : Not been possible to do as much maintenance on this vehicle as others since driver is assistant cook and principal scrounger. Front near-side wing damaged and lamp missing.

Ford 10-cwt.

Mileage : as logged. 5097.2.

Chassis : Good.

Springs : Good.

Tyres : Fair. One good spare available plus buckshee tube.

Battery : Needs draining and new distilled water.

General : Vehicle is more subject to boiling than others but otherwise very good.

15 DEC. 41   *With 5th N.Z. Bde. in front of Gazala*

Just as we were leaving 13th Corps this morning, ran into Capt. Kim Munday and his party of war correspondents—Alex Clifford, *Daily Mail,* Alan Moorehead, *Daily Express,* and Busvine, *Chicago Times.* They seem not to have been in our sector for some little time.

Reached 5th N.Z. Bde. to find that the Wops are still holding out in front of them and the Polish Bde. had moved in on their (the N.Z.) left with the 4th Ind. Div. in their old position on the extreme left flank. They were just teeing up an attack in which the Poles were to join.

The whole enemy position here is stronger than one at first supposed, and in some strong-points which have been taken there is evidence that the position was prepared months ago ; guns have concrete emplacements, for example, and the trench systems are good and extensive. The whole area as one sees it on the map, now that we know more or less the enemy dispositions, proves to be a carefully planned one with a pukka perimeter defence and all.

The Boche armour (estimated 70 tanks of both 21st and 15th Panzer Divs.) is located in their Rear Centre and the position immediately in front here is held by Pavia ; the strange thing is the Wop prisoners' claim that there are no Boche infantry and that they took all the available transport and shoved off yesterday. This would look as if the line might give pretty soon and the Boche knows he cannot hold us and is making the Wops do the rearguard fighting. Yet, as I say, the position is a very strong one, and one supposes it could be held by good troops, provided their L. of C. was intact, for some time to come. That, I think, is where the shoe pinches. We are astride his L. of C. (in the desert, that is) and the R.A.F. is making the main coast road almost untenable except at night.

And, of course, the position is very open to outflanking on its left as we face it and where the 4th Ind. Div. is located.

The N.Z. Bn. has not been able to get any further forward along the road : the Italians have some fairly large guns and there is said to be a stiff anti-tank obstacle. They'll hold on to the road until the last moment, that is certain. But all the time we are hammering them and giving them no peace. The attack going in now is designed to secure some high ground which will probably enable us to enfilade part of their right flank in this sector.

Noticed that our people have buried all the Wops who were lying around here when we left, and that quite a lot of the equipment has been removed. Many more guns have come up and a most decent barrage is just beginning ; should not like to be at the other end of it.

On the way down here we went through a shot-up Wop position previously unnoticed ; must have been most of the people cleaned up by the Maoris in their original advance up here. Among other odds and ends of use to us, found a box of carpenter's tools with some most splendid things in the way of breast drills and so on ; will make a most welcome addition to my workshop.

16 DEC. 41 *With Army Tank Bde. adjoining 4th Indian Div.*

As we left the N.Z. people, many prisoners (Wops) were wending in monotonous lines into the camp.

Went across to the Polish Bde., slap into a storm of shellfire which made everyone hop smartly into some not very good slit-trenches. The Poles had quite a good attack yesterday, they said, but were most disappointed in finding Wops and not Boche fighting them.

What deep-seated, burning, bitter hatred they have for the Boche. It is a thing grim and sombre to behold.

Their Brigade Major spotted Matt Halton's Canadian

shoulder titles and greeted him like a lost brother, it appearing that he was once Polish consul in Winnipeg. They gassed away for damned nearly twenty minutes without anyone else getting a word in sideways and completely oblivious to the fact that the shelling, which had temporarily dropped off, was creeping back again and liable to drop slick on them instantly.

I prised Matt away and set a course for 4th Ind. Div. Before coming up with them, we ran into A.T.B., who told us that we had missed two terrific battles and that he had lost a number of tanks, while the Buffs and an R.A. Battery had suffered heavily.

The plain fact appeared to be that the Boche had thrown everything into a series of violent counter-attacks on our left flank—the Indians—hoping to smash them and turn our line while the Wops held on to the immediate coastal sector.

Well, they failed. Our fellows were too good for them just as they had been at Sidi Omar. One tries to look at it objectively, and this is the only answer. There were heavy casualties on our side; and heavier on theirs. And when the force of their attacks was spent, we still were able to get after them.

From Div., filled in the picture more fully. The Boche had flung the best part of his armoured forces first at Bde., who had with them a grand Field Regt. R.A. An old friend—" Sparks," Signals Officer of Bde.—was up with the guns with his transmitting truck. The Boche came on in a series of charges in the tanks, supported by artillery on half-track vehicles and lorried infantry. The Fd. Regt. adopted their usual tactics of holding fire until the last moment, and the anti-tank guns and Bofors teams did the same. It was the hell of a party. The Boche tried a " one by one " game—concentrating all their fire on one troop and trying to knock it out before switching to the next.

In one troop all the gunners were knocked out and the officers manned the guns until they were wounded. Pretty nearly all the Battery had a wound of some sort. " Sparks " got a direct hit from a tank on his truck, but the transmitter still worked, so he carried on until the last minute. Then, when it was of no use to stay longer, he closed down the transmitter, put a couple of rounds through it, and hopped off, running three miles before he got a lift on a truck.

A liaison officer who was knocking about in his American " Jeeps " car did some grand work collecting wounded chaps and piling them on to his tiny vehicle. Even when all his tyres were punctured he drove on and got the fellows away.

The Boche pressed home the attack for all they were worth, but the 7th were too much for them. They sheered off very much the worse for wear.

At this time a Bde., with the Buffs and Artillery, had pushed forward very strongly and now lay like a rapier in the heart of the enemy's R. flank.

Early the next day the Boche massed his forces once more. Again he had a composite force of tanks, guns and lorried infantry—the 105th Lorried Infantry Regt. The Buffs had a small number of I-tanks with them.

The battle that followed was one of the fiercest of the campaign. As grim and unrelenting as anything fought in the Sidi Rezegh area or at Sidi Omar. One after another the guns of the Field Regt. were knocked out, while they, on their part, smashed tank after tank over open sights, ripped great holes in the advancing infantry and knocked out vehicles bringing up fresh troops. The Buffs fought with the utmost gallantry and, as was seen later, completely annihilated the 105th Lorried Infty. Regt.

Tom Rowe, Staff Capt. at 7th Bde., told us that the Buffs Commanding Officer remained at his wireless transmitter until the very last moment, passing back information as to the progress of the battle and directing his own troops. Finally, most of the Buffs and a Field Regt. were overrun. The C.O., through his transmitter, told the Bde. H.Q. that he had three of our I-tanks about him in phalanx and that they were firing everything they had got; then he said, "The Boche tanks are coming towards me now; I think this will probably be my last transmission."   There was silence, followed by a loud crash as someone put a bullet through the transmitter so that it should not fall whole into enemy hands.

A large number of the Buffs were taken prisoner; unhappy thought. But they had done their work. An intercepted enemy transmission showed that. The Boche were told to attack again with the 105th Lorried Infty. Regt., and the reply was that this was not possible since that Regt. no longer existed.

Since these two great battles, the enemy has still been active, but he is so weakened that he is unable to launch any further full scale attack at this stage. Our own troops are pressing him all the time and now the Brig. says we plan to fling the 32nd Army Tank Bde., weakened by losses to the 4th Bn. but still strong and with fresh tanks on the way up, at the enemy line, while the 4th Armoured Bde. sweep round and in behind. To-morrow should be a great day. The General (did not have a chance to see him) is insistent that the enemy will break.

The sun has gone down now and I must attend to dinner. We shall toast the Buffs in stew, and hope that we can get forward quickly enough to-morrow to recapture those who were taken prisoner.

17 DEC. 41   *With 7th Infty. Bde. approaching Derna*

Oh, it has been a great day; a great day. We have advanced by my speedometer 45.7 miles, and now, with a fighter sweep filling the sky above us, we are leaguering for the night.

Overnight we planned to move to the R. flank again as soon as the big attack was launched, but before breakfast I went across to Div. H.Q. and found everyone packing up and getting on the move. The enemy had withdrawn during the night all along the line, and the first recce. plane reports showed that his transport was haring for Derna on the R. flank and Mekili on the L. flank.

Shot back to our little camp, broke the news and got everyone giving a hand to pack and be off. There was just time for a hurried check over, and then we went right through the Div. to fetch up with the 7th Bde. once more, pay quick compliments to the Brig. and B.M. Peter Hughes, and then start on the great advance.

It has been thrilling to come so far and fast after so many ups and downs. We passed through the Buffs' position and saluted those happy warriors as we did so. Saw many of the tanks knocked out in those great battles and also two tractor-drawn-field-guns, burned and twisted wrecks. On and on and on we went, the Bde. streaming out behind us like a huge armada of destroyers, each vehicle with its own little bow wave of dust and larger wake of churned-up sand. The going was fine for most of the way, until we were about 30 kilometres due West of Tmimi, when it changed abruptly and became stony. The armoured cars ahead constantly wirelessed back messages of the state of affairs ; they did their damnedest to catch up with the Boche, but he had got a long start and only occasionally were they able to smarten up his tail. Passed any number of broken-down and knocked-out lorries—one, a whacking great ammunition truck, was blazing most magnificently and shells were exploding on it with great bangs and roars, flinging burning chunks high in the air—and two Mk. III Boche tanks and one Wop M.13 ; the Wop caught fire as we passed it.

There were no halts for food ; we just munched an occasional biscuit and piece of bully or some chocolate to stave off the worst pangs.

Passed through an old British petrol refuelling point— a reminder of last year's advance—and then came into some surprising country. We have for so long seen nothing but sand and dried mud and rubble and unending flatness, that the sight which broke upon the view made one stare unbelievingly. There were gentle slopes, semi-wooded with small *green* bushes, and in one small wadi some rain-water. A few trucks even got stuck in the mud in this wadi ; just imagine it—stuck in the mud ! My driver laughed at the sight a little too uproariously, so I rebuked him on the quite proper grounds that he should not laugh at a comrade's downfall ; he said, " But honestly, sir, it is the funniest thing I've ever seen." And maybe it was.

One would have thought that the enemy would bomb us and try to hamper our advance ; but they did not. The only planes we have seen this day bore British markings.

Have just listened-in to the B.B.C. news. It always seems a little odd to hear someone in London telling about the deeds in Libya.

Speculation to-night on where the Boche will make his next stand. One imagines this must surely be Derna on the coast and Mekili in the desert, for, after these two places, there isn't much where a good defence could be put up. It all depends on how quickly we get after him and upon the strength of his remaining armoured forces.

Just before turning in, heard that the 4th A.B. had contacted some enemy tanks and guns plus lorried infantry near Mekili.

18 DEC. 41　　　　　　　　　　　　　　*Before Derna*

Well, I am probably quite wrong, but I fancy we have

been too quick for the enemy and that he is hopping it for all he is worth to Benghazi.

To-day's advance had been arduous and very tough on the transport. We were up and away at the very first sparrow's cough, and we made the newly-built Derna perimeter road at Martuba by latish afternoon. The going was fair to begin with; then it deteriorated quickly, and soon we were struggling hard to keep formation in a vast mass of wadis that were sometimes a hundred and more feet deep. I prayed hard that the trucks would stand up to it and nursed them all carefully through the jumbled masses of rock and over old torrent beds. Number Three truck boiled constantly and used up the devil of a lot of water, dammit.

But finally the Bde. halted just short of Martuba (its second objective, the first being Tmimi—though this was washed out when we found that the enemy had vanished) and very soon the Div. Cmndr. came charging up—just in time to be machine-gunned by some wretched yellow-nosed Me.'s—very full of beans.

The New Zealanders, who were advancing on our R. along the line of the road and the immediate top of the escarpment, have been left far behind and we have the battlefield to ourselves. Ahead the C.I.H. are sending their Bren carriers nosing towards Derna through a narrow and precipitous gorge. The Royal Sussex are on our right and they are going to make good the aerodrome, on which, as I can see through the glasses, there appear to be dozens of grounded planes—most of them burned out or smashed.

It is all enormously exciting, since we do not quite know whether there is going to be a battle or not.

LATER

Left the Bde. and came on with the carriers. Sculled around and found that the Sussex had secured the aerodrome—a very big and well-equipped one—finding lots of planes but no enemy. Just at last light eight Boche Junkers transport machines swooped down to land on the drome (some of their vaunted staff wallahs seem to have slipped up a bit), and the Sussex with the aid of some anti-tank guns knocked out six of them; the other two managed to get off. As all this was happening, half a dozen lorries appeared from nowhere and hared across the aerodrome on the good road which runs through it. The gunners took their time and blasted hell out of all of them; one was carrying ammunition; a 25-pdr. shell hit it fair and square and there wasn't any lorry any more.

We hear the aerodrome is mined in places. Now it is after dark, and we have made camp near some old Arab tombs in which, from obvious bits of evidence about, some Wops have been living for some time. Goodness knows what has happened to them. Thought possibly they might be still in the largest of the tombs—quite an extensive thing running many yds. underground—so bellowed for them to come out and loosed off a burst from my tommy-gun just to show there was no ill-feeling. Anyhow, nothing happened.

There is a little banging about in the direction of Derna, but nothing much. We shall be in there to-morrow for a ducat.

19 DEC. 41   *With Rear Army nr. Tobruk*

We moved forward cautiously on Derna through the narrow gorge and came slap upon the aerodrome. Gosh ! planes of every sort all over the place and also some big gliders which, I gather, they have been using to bring in troops and supplies. Bombs by the thousand, and also a great many discarded auxiliary petrol tanks for planes. They really must have gone off in a hurry, for much of the complicated-looking wireless equipment appeared undamaged. There was a line of mines across our path, but negotiated these all right and pushed on along the main road which leads down into Derna.

We were stopped just before getting to the hair-pin bends and told that there was a big road block—the retreating enemy had blown the road. Told my chickens that we could not get down for a few hours, and after a conference it was decided that Matt Halton and I should drive back to Army with the despatches and return as quickly as possible. The risk was worth it, though the journey was more than 150 miles by my reckoning.

While they were writing, I wandered on and snooped around the road and saw Derna lying peacefully below— about 600 feet, I should think. There was no shipping in the harbour. Through the glasses could see that the place was, to all intents and purposes, abandoned. Doors open and flapping miserably in the wind, windows smashed, no plume of smoke from any chimney. It seemed undamaged to any great extent and really, in the bright, cold sunlight, looked quite lovely.

Set off with the despatches soon after 10.00 hrs., passed through the aerodrome and lost count of the number of damaged planes; found two apparently undamaged A.A. guns, their tractors off the road and their dead crews lying beside them. Quite a number of Italian dead, but no Boche so far as I could see. Met Ronnie Noble, film cameraman of *Universal*, on the road and told him to push on and try to get in for the actual entry into Derna. Thereafter met at least four more parties of P.R. people. Matt said, " It is rather nice to be going back when everyone else is just creeping forward, don't you think ? " And really it *was* rather a pleasant feeling. Just before entering Tobruk, having made darned good time, had a blowout that cost us two precious hours and prevented us getting to Adv. Army

H.Q. Nothing could be more infuriating. However, these things are sent to try us, so now we are installed with Rear Army H.Q. and have been most kindly supplied with a shave and a wash and somewhere to lay our weary heads. We push on to Adv. Army H.Q. at first light and must then do our best to get back to Derna.

20 DEC. 41   *At Adv. Army H.Q. nr. Tobruk*

I was so tired last night that I did not record all I might about the journey from Derna ; I particularly remember the simply vast dump (Wop) at Gazala ; no wonder those blighters hung on there and made such a fuss. It was the biggest dump I had ever seen anywhere, and the material thus fallen to us must be tremendously important.

Also remember seeing, near a place called Umm el Rzem, half a dozen Italian ammunition lorries which had been machine-gunned and bombed by the R.A.F. It was a horrid spectacle.

Hell of a dust-storm is holding us up here now. Sorted out kit and bits and pieces collected during the campaign, and had a most magnificent wash in *hot* water —incredible luxury. Gave G.S.I. what information I could about Derna, and gather from them and other people that they feel things are going pretty well for us one way and another. I should jolly well think they are !

It has been difficult enough all along to keep track of events and see the campaign as a whole, but it is even more tricky now. We have at least five separate columns driving into the enemy flank at various points.

Sam Brewer turned up by air during the day and comes back with me to-morrow.

Some excellent chianti has appeared from somewhere and, bless my soul, I must say that it is very pleasant to close all the tent flaps against the dust-storm and relax over a mug of it.

21 DEC. 41 *Derna P.R. H.Q.*

A fast journey here to find most of the other parties had arrived and set up H.Q. in this very luxurious (at one time) house, which is said to have been the residence of General Graziani.

The Indians are pushing on along the road and have taken Giovanni Berta—about 35 km. along the main road.

Very little indeed left in this place ; they must have begun evacuating at least a week ago to have stripped the place so thoroughly. There is scarcely a stick of furniture in this house. And, unfortunately, the water is cut off, otherwise one could take a bath in one of the half-dozen bathrooms available.

I have a chance to reorganise somewhat before going on, and have completed the inventory to-day. Our 3-tonner hauled in, and the mechanics at once got to work seeing over the vehicles and patching them up. They look very different from the pristine fleet I sent off from Bagush more than a month ago.

My speedometer records a total mileage of 1354.7—quite a bit of running about.

22 DEC. 41 *Albergo Cyrene—Cyrene*

Up early after a very uncomfortable night. Must have been the fact that we were sleeping in a house—something I have not done for months—and also there were dozens of howling dogs making the night hideous.

The transport wanted a devil of a lot of seeing to, and it was very late before we got away from Mister Graziani's place—arranging, perhaps optimistically, for someone to pick up our despatches at Barce to-morrow.

Weather has been absolutely frightful all day : alternate bursts of sunshine and the most violent rainstorms. The country is quite lovely, when one can see it through the blinding rain ; heavily wooded, hilly, and so marvellously green. Called in on 5th Bde. 4th Ind. Div. to say how-d'ye-do. They are headquartered at Giovanni Berta—a poorly pretentious place which looked its drab, stucco worst in the mist and rain—and stated that their armoured-car patrols had instructions to proceed 60 m. along both roads leading to Barce and that so far they had reported no opposition, although it is believed that both roads are blown and may be lightly defended at the blocks.

We battled on to Cyrene, wrapt in mist and rain, very high, set among the most wonderful Roman ruins, that touch a chord of sadness in one's heart : they are so enduring and beautiful. Here we are camped, out of the rain, in a vast, barrack-like tourist hotel which has been so completely stripped that even the panelling on the walls has been ripped off. There isn't a whole window anywhere ; an awful shambles.

The Italian colonists' houses we passed on the road here were poor, mass-produced, cubist-looking affairs set whitely in the red soil and yellow rocky outcrops. Some of the colonists have remained—white flags (now almost a national emblem, surely) fluttering raggedly in the wind and rain.

A few of them gave an automatic Fascist salute, and then tried hard to alter it into a British Army one.

Scrounging in and around the hotel, found a little fuel oil, some lubricating oil and a number of British tyres. One of the tyres fits my truck and is most welcome.

The amount of damage done in the hotel is simply fantastic. Everything has been destroyed—everything. Yet, behold ! the electric light works. I don't know how or why or anything about it ; the plain fact is that it works, and here I am—able to write in comfort, instead of by torchlight as usual.

There are no troops here—they seem to have bypassed the place, leaving only a small anti-tank and artillery crowd on the outskirts of the village—so there has been a long procession of local chiefs, servants, egg-sellers, dirty children and dirtier women, police and what-have-you, coming in to make their courtesies and ask for favours.

Faced with this sort of position, one is a little flummoxed, it being no part of my job to handle the problems they present. However, I like to think that they all went away satisfied in some measure—except the children, that is ; they are hungry, cold and wet ; and they are in droves outside, the rain notwithstanding.

A check-up (rather hurried) showed that we are running short of food. Water is all right and should, in any case, no longer be the old-man-of-the-sea as in the past. Petrol is very short indeed. I estimate that I can just about make Barce and no more, but am prepared to take a chance on picking up some there. Also, we observe that it is getting near Christmas-time and have promised ourselves that we shall spend that holy day in Benghazi, if it be humanly possible. *And* (what a big *and*!) some weeks ago we sent a list to the C.O. in Cairo ; a list of all the things we'd like to have for Christmas dinner ; with an open cheque. We wonder very much whether they will get the stuff up to us. It will be a good effort if they do, for we hop about all over the place and must be difficult to find. Still, we hope.

23 DEC. 41 *Albergo Cyrene—Cyrene*

On to Luigi Razza, where we spotted a whole lot of tanks half-hidden in the bushes at the side of the road. Got out to investigate and counted 14 M.13's, all new and undamaged except that, in some cases, the guns had been immobilised. It seemed to be some sort of workshops H.Q. for the Ariete Div., for there were a number of buildings about. While snooping around these, some sportsman opened up on me with a machine-gun. Could not see who or what he was, and after a fruitless search decided to shove on. Soon after, we met the road block. Came up with three South African armoured cars in the Wadi Cufa (not marked on map but locals say this is the name), and saw the road had been very effectively blown. The S.A. people reckoned it would take them 8 hrs. to clear the thing, so there was nothing for it but to return along the way we had come.

This was a bad blow, as the journey to Luigi Razza had eaten into my petrol and I doubted whether, even with my secret reserve, we could do the journey back to Cyrene and then on again by the lower road to Barce.

Going back we picked up three airmen who had been shot down in Barce. They were hungry and simply eaten up with socking great fleas.

At Cyrene, went up to the hotel again and fed and watered our three Air Force wallahs, and also met up with Freeman, a new P.R. officer, who had been on his way to Barce to collect our despatches, heard we were in Cyrene and so looked in ; decent piece of luck.

The problem—of course—was petrol.

I have enough for an 80 m. run for all three trucks—and Barce is 70 m. away. Salusbury and Jacob voted against going on and preferred to wait for petrol convoys to come through, so that we could be sure of getting to Barce and being able to push on to Benghazi. Sam Brewer and Matt Halton voted for going on and taking a chance on some petrol at Barce. I threw in my deciding vote with them—purely playing my luck and because I hate sitting still, anyway.

The Christmas dinner came up for discussion, and we are all sending up a prayer this night that it may catch us up. I should particularly like the men to have a decent dinner; they have been very good and have never failed to come up to scratch.

CHRISTMAS EVE 1941   *Albergo Moderne—Barce*

A lucky, lucky day. Instead of going straight off to Barce, as we had decided overnight, I decided to use up a *very* secret 4 gallons of juice and hop down back to Giovanni Berta where 4th Ind. Div. were installed, get my map marked, scrounge some petrol if possible, and also see if there was any news of the Christmas stuff.

There was no petrol to be had and no news of our goodies. So I set off back, and then spotted a giant petrol tanker (Wop) by the side of the road. Cannot think how I missed it before. Got out and was crawling over it trying to see if it had any juice in it when a loud hooting from the road made me damned nearly fall off the top of the thing. It was Munroe, a P.R. Officer, who was not only bringing us petrol but also had the *boxes*—£21 worth of stuff, representing our blank cheque.

Back like a flash to Cyrene and in less than an hour we were off to Barce. The road was good. It had been blown in one place—very ineffectually—and the whole way along there was knocked-out Wop and Boche transport of one sort or another. The Air Force seem to have done themselves proud along here.

Barce lies on the coastal plain. A dirty, disappointing little place after what one had heard about it. The hotel was semi-functioning; no light (though I have a scrounged candle in the room at the moment), no water or means of cooking; the bar was open, but I have not had time to do anything about it. Got the men and transport fixed up, and then cooked a meal in an empty house, not liking Barce one little bit.

All—or most—of the correspondents are here and intending to push on to Benghazi to-morrow. So, with any luck, it will be Benghazi on Christmas Day as we had planned. It seems that our old friends, 7th Infty. Bde., intend to be there at roughly the same time. They have been resting for a few days at Derna.

Matt Halton is sharing this room with me, so we shall chinwag away the rest of Christmas Eve.

CHRISTMAS DAY 1941   *Benghazi*

An early start, but a C.I.H. convoy and some punctures rather held us up. Made Benghazi, a weird, straggling, dirty place. It has been bombed to hell—especially the harbour, which really is a shambles. The docks are full of sunken ships ; great masses of masonry have been tossed by bomb explosions high and far and wide ; all the buildings along the quaysides are roofless, empty, blackened shells.

We managed to find a block of flats which was not too badly damaged, and now have set up home and had a really fine Christmas dinner. There is no light or water at the moment, but we scared up candles and lamps of one sort or another, moved in all my precious stoves and pots and pans and our food store.

Opening the Christmas boxes was a great ceremony, and very soon we had a magnificent sideboard of liquor, which, I may say, attracted a good deal of attention from neighbouring parties.

I cooked dinner. We had no turkey, but Fred Bayliss turned up late in the evening with half the carcase of one, and we all sat around slicing bits off it and gnawing the bones over drinks. My three drivers, shaved and with their hair brushed, looked very smart, and we took turns in serving them.

The dinner :—
  A huge tinned ham (fabulously expensive)
  Mashed potatoes with masses of margarine
  Sweet corn garnished with tiny sardines
  Sliced bully with button mushrooms
  Sauerkraut
  Piles of boiled onions
  Asparagus
  M & V (Boche)
  Oranges and nuts
  Tinned Christmas pudding.

Some fathead spilled petrol on the cigars, so they weren't too good ; but, dammit, we had to smoke them after having got them nearly 700 miles.

Of course, we poured brandy over the Christmas pudding and piped it in, also the ham.

There was much singing and noise. Noble obliged on his mouth-organ, Keating sang some Irish songs, Downs sang some good old maudlin stuff about grey-haired mothers and grey-roofed cottages, Pinney sang a tough song about subalterns, and, all in all, things went with a swing.

One thought very much of home, but by general agreement the subject was taboo.

Our forward troops are contacting the enemy's rear-guard at Agedabia, but we have moved so far and so fast in the last few days that I doubt if we shall push on much further for a little while. Rather less than 100 British sick were found in the hospital here, and there are all sorts of types knocking about who managed to escape and hide when the Boche and Wops evacuated the place. One gathers that the Boche did themselves rather well while they were here ; signs of every sort in German are all over the place.

It is fairly late now. There are social calls to make on some of the other parties ; one must be quite meticulous about saying " Happy Christmas " to *every*one—even the couple of scared-looking Christian Brothers across the way.

26 Dec. 41   *Benghazi*

Mosquitoes attacked me all through the night, dive-bombing my forehead ; so this morning I have a head-ache, just as on all the other mornings of Boxing Day that I can remember.

Had a grand breakfast and actually drank coffee out of china cups, which Scrounger Downs produced. Ambled round the town and airport. A great many crashed and otherwise damaged planes at Binina Main—well over a hundred, I should think. Axis air losses in this campaign must be fantastically high, especially those destroyed on the ground by various means.

Feeling rather lazy and weary, but must use the time at my disposal to check everything over and get the vehicles maintenanced. May take my own truck out to-morrow towards Agedabia and see what the form is there ; the other two trucks can be left behind here, and the place used as a base. Getting despatches back is going to be the difficulty until we start using the airfield here, but we are arranging a Don R. service. Called in at the hospital and saw a lot of our fellows—most of them look pretty seedy ; they say that the Wops treated them very badly, but that the Germans were not so bad. Heard that the Buffs captured at Gazala had passed through the P.O.W. camp. Got news also of Eddie Ward, *B.B.C.,* Harold Denny, *New York Times,* and Anderson, *U.P.* They all arrived on Nov. 26 ; Anderson and Denny were shunted out two days later, but Ward, who speaks good Italian, remained behind for a week helping the South African Major who was Prisoner Camp Commandant. He said all three fellows were as cheerful as the circumstances allowed when they arrived, and that Eddie Ward was " full of guts and worked all day like a slave to help the men who were wounded and sick."

Some time back, while with 7th Armd. Div., I heard what little was known about their capture. Apparently the General went out on a recce. in an area known to hold a good few enemy. The three correspondents—Ward in his own truck full of sound apparatus, etc., and Denny and Anderson in one of the P.R. trucks—decided to follow the General, although Michael Crighton, Intelligence Officer 7th A.D., suggested it might be a bit risky and unwise. However, they seemed to think they would be all right and followed on after the General's truck, some good distance behind it. They were not seen again, and the assumption is that they had a breakdown and were then taken unawares and popped into the bag.

The S.A. Major did not know any further details nor had Eddie left any note behind with him. He said conditions were very bad in the P.O.W. camp, which was designed to hold only 400 and into which at one time 4,000 men were crammed.

27 Dec. 41   *Benghazi*

Sam Brewer and Alaric Jacob departed for 8th Army to-day, intending to go on back to Cairo for a rest and refit. That leaves me with only Matt Halton and Fred Salusbury. Took my truck out and pushed down the main road towards Agedabia. A dreadful day—high wind, heavy rain, and a thick layer of the most treacherous mud on the road. We went as far as Ghemines before meeting up with part of a Support Group. They had not any news, but thought the road was all right for some distance ahead, although there were enemy pockets reported. Went on to Magrun, where there is a large landing ground. Quite a lot of burned-out troop-carrier planes and a couple of badly shot-up Stukas, but not much else. The weather grew progressively worse, and then the truck began to cough and splutter, so we had to turn back.

Looked in at Bde. H.Q. to hear that a search of the city, still in progress, had uncovered an extremely large R.E. stores dump, £1,000,000 worth of medical supplies, some still uncrated, A.A. guns and predictors, 100,000 gals. of petrol and oil in underground containers, and— lots and lots of fresh meat in a refrigerator store. Coughed gently and significantly at the mention of this last, and was rewarded by the promise of a joint to-morrow.

The enemy seems to be digging-in a bit at Agedabia, and has a lot of guns there ; his armour is lurking in the background, refurbished, it seems, and probably rein- forced through Tripoli and possibly one or two other places along the coast. He quite sees that the very bad weather and our very extended lines of communication prevent us from winkling him out immediately, and is taking the opportunity to get as much of his stuff away in safety as he can.

28 DEC. 41   *Benghazi*

A horrid day. The rain has been pelting down and the wind is unceasing. My forehead, bitten by mosquitoes, looks like a turnip field, and I'm generally feeling off colour. Houses and streets and things depress me, anyhow, after nearly eight solid months in the desert.

We got our leg of beef, and Woodward, a most expert butcher, produced some really first-rate steaks off it which I fried. Everyone said they were delicious, and certainly it was pleasant to eat fresh meat again after so much bully and tinned stuff.

Forward there is not a great deal happening, but the 22nd Armd. Bde. is sculling around and will probably bump the Boche tanks very soon.

29 DEC. 41 *Benghazi*

Major Oakshott, Second-in-Command, who arrived here yesterday, thinks I should go back to Cairo for a rest while things are quieter here, and it was finally decided that I take Halton and Salusbury back *via* Bardia, which, it seems, we shall clean up pretty soon. Hate the idea of leaving the front, but have to confess the logic of Major Oakshott's argument.

30 DEC. 41 *El Adem Aerodrome*

At the last moment it seemed there were two places on a Bombay leaving Benghazi and, as Salusbury did not care about flying back, it was decided that Halton and I should go ; I turned my transport over to Ely. Reached this place at 10.00 hrs. to find that the plane was not going any further. So waited about, cold and hungry, all day for another machine—which did not arrive. So now we are installed for the night in a Bombay bomber.

31 DEC. 41 *Shepheard's Hotel, Cairo*

Reached here at dark, having got a lift around 14.00 hrs. in a very fast American plane. It seems almost criminal to have got back in such a short space of time. It was very easy to follow the route from El Adem, and a great sense of nostalgia and sadness gripped me as I looked down and saw transport crawling through the sand below, each with its tiny wake of dust.

Here it is New Year's Eve and everyone is very bright and merry. I find it difficult to join in, and suppose I am tired or something. Anyhow, I let the barber loose on myself for an hour, have taken a bath ; and now, in bed, compose myself to take a glass of wine with Matt, who also feels rather low and flat.

Waiting for me here was a parcel containing a çopy of

Rupert Brooke's poems : a Christmas present from my wife.

And because the old year is passing now and the new year is coming in, I thought of those of our people who had died in battle, in a great battle, to their unending, undying honour. For most of them there is a grave in the sand, perhaps a few rocks piled over them, their names in hurried pencil-scrawl upon a cross made of petrol cases. For some there is no cross : only a mound of sand that soon the wind will soften and gently erase. But for them all—

" Blow out, you bugles, over the rich Dead !
   There's none of these so lonely and poor of old,
   But, dying, has made us rarer gifts than gold.
These laid the world away ; poured out the red
Sweet wine of youth ; gave up the years to be
   Of work and joy, and that unhoped serene,
   That men call age ; and those who would have been,
Their sons, they gave, their immortality."

CROWN COPYRIGHT RESERVED

First Published 1942

To be purchased from His Majesty's Stationery Office at York House, Kingsway, London, W.C.2 ; 120 George Street, Edinburgh 2 ; 39–41 King Street, Manchester 2 ; 1 St. Andrew's Crescent, Cardiff ; 80 Chichester Street, Belfast ; or through any bookseller.

Price 6*d.* net or 20*s.* for 50 copies. S.O. Code No. 70-395*

*Made and Printed in Great Britain by the Whitefriars Press Limited
London and Tonbridge*

Cover Printed by Fosh & Cross Limited